THE VARIETIES
OF GROUNDED
THEORY

SAGE SWIFTS

In 1976 SAGE published a series of short 'university papers', which led to the publication of the QASS series (or the 'little green books' as they became known to researchers). More than 40 years since the release of the first 'little green book', SAGE is delighted to offer a new series of swift, short and topical pieces in the ever-growing digital environment.

SAGE *Swifts* offer authors a new channel for academic research with the freedom to deliver work outside the conventional length of journal articles. The series aims to give authors speedy access to academic audiences through digital first publication, space to explore ideas thoroughly, yet at a length which can be readily digested, and the quality stamp and reassurance of peer-review.

THE VARIETIES
OF GROUNDED
THEORY

ANTONY BRYANT

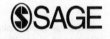

Los Angeles | London | New Delhi
Singapore | Washington DC | Melbourne

Los Angeles | London | New Delhi
Singapore | Washington DC | Melbourne

SAGE Publications Ltd
1 Oliver's Yard
55 City Road
London EC1Y 1SP

SAGE Publications Inc.
2455 Teller Road
Thousand Oaks, California 91320

SAGE Publications India Pvt Ltd
B 1/I 1 Mohan Cooperative Industrial Area
Mathura Road
New Delhi 110 044

SAGE Publications Asia-Pacific Pte Ltd
3 Church Street
#10-04 Samsung Hub
Singapore 049483

Editor: Jai Seaman
Editorial assistant: Lauren Jacobs
Production editor: Victoria Nicholas
Copyeditor: Sarah Bury
Proofreader: Jill Birch
Marketing manager: Susheel Gokarakonda
Cover design: Shaun Mercier
Typeset by: C&M Digitals (P) Ltd, Chennai, India
Printed in the UK

Library of Congress Control Number: 2018963668

British Library Cataloguing in Publication data

A catalogue record for this book is available from the British Library

ISBN 978-1-5264-7431-5
Web PDF 978-1-5264-7976-1

At SAGE we take sustainability seriously. Most of our products are printed in the UK using responsibly sourced papers and boards. When we print overseas we ensure sustainable papers are used as measured by the PREPS grading system. We undertake an annual audit to monitor our sustainability.

CONTENTS

ABOUT THE AUTHOR

Antony Bryant is currently Professor of Informatics at Leeds Beckett University, Leeds, UK.

He has written and taught extensively on research methods, with a particular interest in qualitative research methods, and the Grounded Theory Method in particular. His book *Grounded Theory and Grounded Theorizing: Pragmatism in Research Practice* was recently published by Oxford University Press (2017). He is Senior Editor of *The SAGE Handbook of Grounded Theory* (Sage, 2007) and *The SAGE Handbook of Current Developments in Grounded Theory* – both co-edited with Kathy Charmaz (Sage, 2019).

He has supervised over 50 doctoral students, and examined many others, in topics including formal specification of software systems, development of quality and maturity frameworks, new forms of business modelling, and various aspects of e-government and e-democracy.

He is currently working with Professor Frank Land, who worked on the first commercial computer (LEO 1951), and was also the first UK Professor of Information Systems, on a series of 'conversations' planned for publication that will cover issues in the development and impact of computer technology since the 1950s.

ACKNOWLEDGEMENTS

Publication of *The Sage Handbook of Grounded Theory* and *The Sage Handbook of Current Developments in Grounded Theory* would not have been possible without Kathy Charmaz. The contributors were almost entirely her recommendations, and almost all those approached readily accepted the invitation largely because of her involvement. She has worked with GTM almost since its inception, and her contribution to the development and flourishing of the method is unique and incomparable.

This discussion of the varieties of GTM was initially intended to be a joint editorial essay for *Current Developments*, and Kathy offered useful advice on earlier drafts. Her influence should be obvious throughout the discussion, although I know there will be many aspects about which she will have reservations. It was at her suggestion that I publish this as sole author. Given its length, Jai Seaman, Senior Commissioning Editor at Sage, recommended that the essay be published separately in the *Swifts* series, to appear prior to *Current Developments* itself. Jai, Lauren Jacobs, and their colleagues at Sage have been enormously supportive in moving both *Varieties* and *Current Developments* to publication.

I must also thank all contributors to *Current Developments*. Their chapters provided the starting point for much of what follows, affording me the opportunity for an idiosyncratic, but I hope informed and respectful, discussion on GTM and several important and related topics. I have learned a great deal from all the chapters, and from extended email exchanges with many of the contributors. I look forward to these exchanges continuing in the future.

≮≮

INTRODUCTION AND RATIONALE

This monograph was initially written as an introduction to what was envisaged as a revised and updated version of *The SAGE Handbook of Grounded Theory* (Bryant and Charmaz, 2007a). In preparation Kathy Charmaz and I contacted contributors to the earlier volume, inviting them to submit revised versions of their work, or to consider new material, possibly but not necessarily related to their earlier chapter. We also invited submissions from authors not included in 2007. The result is a volume comprising 31 chapters with more than 75% of the material being substantively different from the 2007 volume. Since the material in the 2007 volume retains its validity and importance, publishing the new volume as a 'revised' edition would have been misleading. Hence the decision to publish it as *The SAGE Handbook of Current Developments in Grounded Theory* (Bryant and Charmaz, 2019, hereafter *Current Developments*).

The new chapters indicate the range and depth of writing on the Grounded Theory Method (GTM), and the ways in which discussion of research methods has developed and expanded in recent years. I felt that it was important to bring key aspects of all of this to the attention of readers; also to discuss the complexities, interrelationships, and contrasts between the submissions. This necessitated a detailed and considered overview of the material – something far more substantial than an editors' introduction. As the work developed, I sent revised drafts to Kathy, who offered insightful responses and eventually suggested that the material, now over 40,000 words, appear as a chapter solely under my name.

Given its length, and in discussion with Jai Seaman, Senior Commissioning Editor at Sage, it was agreed that the 'chapter' should be revised and published as a separate monograph in the *SAGE Swifts* series, to appear just ahead of *Current Developments*: A precursor heralding the new volume, but which can also be read as a stand-alone publication. (The original title for this chapter/monograph was 'The Varieties of Grounded Theory Experience', evoking William James's *The Varieties of Religious*

Experience (1902), James being one of the founding figures of Pragmatism, a key component of GTM.)

The rich variety of the contributions to *Current Developments* inevitably results in potentially or actually contradictory statements; some relating to GTM itself, others having wider ramifications. I therefore saw my position as Senior Editor as providing the opportunity not only to present some of the key concerns covered by the contributors, but also to take issue with some of them. (NB: References to chapters in *Current Developments* will be indicated in this manner – i.e. CD:NN, where NN is the chapter number. The titles of the individual chapters are listed in Appendix B. In some cases, the actual quote may differ slightly from that in the published version since I have worked from the draft versions dating from mid-2018.)

My discussion of these contributions might be regarded as idiosyncratic, but I hope I have done justice to the nuances and details of the chapters themselves. Some of my ideas developed from comments evoked by early drafts, and were communicated to the contributors, allowing them the opportunity to respond and revise if they so wished. But many others only arose once I had the later versions, and so will come as a surprise to the authors concerned. If this is seen as taking unfair advantage of my role as Senior Editor then I can only apologise, but trust that I have treated people's arguments fairly and given them all due consideration. Moreover, if these do evoke discussion and disagreement, I trust that we can find reasoned and reasonable ways to develop our deliberations in the future.

GTM has always represented a challenge to research orthodoxy, and this shows no sign of abating. *Current Developments* exemplifies and continues this characteristic tendency, offering readers rich insights into current GTM thinking. Vivian Martin (CD:11) identifies a crucial point, noting that 'Flick (2015) observed that many of the challenges that faced qualitative research in the 1980s and 1990s, including concerns with rigor and quality, remain'. But other concerns have arisen, for instance those emanating from the development of computer-based tools, issues around the role of researchers and their interaction with their subjects/participants, and the status of research findings and associated knowledge-claims. For GTM these trends are evident in

- discussions about CAQDAS [Computer Assisted Qualitative Data Analysis Software];
- research in the age of Big Data;[1]

- the nature of abductive reasoning;[2]
- researching across cultures and subcultures;
- and the ways in which researchers can and should relate to issues such as inequality and social justice.

In part, these developments provide opportunities to extend the repertoire available to researchers, but like all innovations they can sometimes side-track or undermine good research practices. In this vein, Martin notes that Flick 'identified trends such as evidence-based research and the rise of big social science projects, with collaborators across departments and institutions, as a threat to small, individual qualitative studies'.

Our introduction to the 2007 volume offered an overview of GTM (Bryant and Charmaz, 2007b), and we also contributed a chapter discussing its historical development, offering an epistemological account of the method's origins and later variants (Bryant and Charmaz, 2007c). The present discussion is designed to serve a different purpose, essentially focusing on the ways in which GTM has developed since 2007, integrating and discussing key points raised in *Current Developments*. Some of these developments are specific to GTM, but many are bound up with issues that impact upon research in general and qualitative approaches in particular. So although closely linked to, and building upon, the chapters in *Current Developments*, this discussion of the varieties of grounded theory offers a complementary and supplementary perspective.

In what follows I address the following issues, in most cases initially relating them to chapters in *Current Developments*:

- A restatement of my view that GTM is best regarded as a 'family of methods', that has flourished and developed, leading to a number of variants that should be regarded as capable of enriching each other, providing the basis for more credible and rigorous research practice in general;
- Discussion of the ways in which GTM can be related to earlier ideas and research, particularly that associated with the Chicago School;
- Clarification of terminology, including GTM-specific terms such as 'code', 'category', and 'concept';
- Some further clarification of the ways in which epistemological and ontological discussions relate to GTM, and vice versa;
- The role of metaphors in characterizing and distinguishing between variants of GTM and researching generally;

- Consideration of the concept of 'abduction' and the ways in which the term is now generally understood, particularly within the context of GTM;
- The impact of technological advances on GTM – particularly CAQDAS and Big Data;
- The paradoxical relationship between GTM and sociology;
- The ways in which writers have developed and enhanced the set of initial, open-ended questions that GTM researchers can consider at the outset of their investigations;
- What is meant by the claim that GTM facilitates the development of a theory, particularly in the light of several criticisms of the method that pose the rhetorical challenge 'Where is the theory in Grounded Theory?';
- Work within GTM that pays specific attention to 'sensitizing issues' such as feminism, race, ethnicity, and indigeneity;
- GTM, Pragmatism and social justice.

These topics should be of interest to anyone wishing to find out more about GTM with a view to using it as part of their research strategy. In general, I have assumed that readers already have some familiarity with GTM, hopefully including Charmaz's *Constructing Grounded Theory* (2014a); by far the best introduction to the method. But for one or two topics, such as abduction, I offer a more detailed exposition, also suggestions for further reading.

I encourage readers to consider the arguments offered here, while also referring to the relevant chapters in *Current Developments*, bearing in mind that my 'reading' may well differ from yours.

Notes

1 Big Data consist of enormous data sets that exceed traditional modes of analysis. Despite multiple challenges in accessing, storing, and managing these data sets, they are increasingly mined for purposes such as improving business practices. See Bryant & Raja, 2014.

2 In brief, abductive reasoning occurs when a researcher cannot explain a finding by invoking theories that account for other patterns in the data. The researcher then considers a range of theoretical explanations and infers what is the best explanation, which he or she then puts through some form of test or validation.

I
GTM – A FAMILY OF VARIANTS

The first generation – Glaser, Strauss, and Quint

In our introductory essay in 2007 (Bryant & Charmaz, 2007b), we described GTM as a 'family of methods', a metaphor that can be construed in several ways, for instance, evoking Tolstoy's opening to *Anna Karenina*: 'All happy families are alike; each unhappy family is unhappy in its own way'. Charmaz also uses the term 'constellation' (Charmaz, 2014a), and others have referred to GTM as an 'umbrella term' or 'framework' (unified or not, as the case may be). Charmaz now avoids the term 'family' because of its connotations, ranging from unwavering commitment to conflict and abuse.

The main rationale for my use of the term 'family' was derived from Wittgenstein's discussion of 'family resemblances':

> we see a complicated network of similarities overlapping and cries-crossing [*sic* criss-crossing]: sometimes overall similarities. I can think of no better expression to characterize these similarities than **family resemblances**; for the various resemblances between members of a family: build, features, colour of eyes, gait, temperament, etc. etc. overlap and cries-cross [*sic* criss-cross] in the same way. (Wittgenstein, n.d., extract from Aphorisms 66 and 67, emphasis in original)

A close reading of this section of Wittgenstein's *Philosophical Investigations* (2001[1953]) indicates that in addition to postulating the concept of 'family resemblances', he was also advocating something akin to the method of constant comparison. Indeed, he uses a phrase that by complete coincidence echoes a key sentiment of Glaser and Strauss.

> 66. Consider for example the proceedings that we call 'games'. I mean board-games, card-games, ball-games, Olympic games, and so on. What is common

to them all? – Don't say: 'There must be something common, or they would not be called "games"' – but look and see whether there is anything common to all. For if you look at them you will not see something that is common to all, but similarities, relationships, and a whole series of them at that. *To repeat: don't think, but look!* (Wittgenstein, n.d., extract from Aphorisms 66, emphasis added)

In similar fashion, a discussion of the ways in which GTM has developed since the 1960s might be understood as a series of relationships and derivations between and across different generations and offspring of the method from its inception. This is not unique to GTM, but a common feature of many methods, and usually a sign of healthy growth and engaging debate. Action Research (AR), for instance, originating in the work of Kurt Lewin and colleagues in the 1930s, has spawned numerous variants. Some of these alternatives clearly derive from AR, incorporating the term itself (e.g. Participatory AR, Community AR, and so on); others do not (e.g. Soft Systems Analysis). Yet they co-exist and provide the basis for new methodological insights, both for those using AR and for others among the wider research community (see Reason & Bradbury-Huang, 2015). For example, Joyce Duckles, George Moses, and Robert Moses (CD:31) depict how community-based participatory action research combined with constructivist grounded theory can contribute to social transformation.

Our concern in 2007 was to explain that the various forms of GTM testified to its importance and vitality, albeit carrying the potential for confusion and raising issues regarding the core aspects of the method. As I will argue below, GTM proponents largely agree on some 'core' or 'essential' characteristics of GTM but differ regarding others. Nonetheless, researchers should never forget that the ultimate significance of a method is how it facilitates developing new and critical insights; something that often involves departing from the well-trodden paths of specific disciplines and common procedures. This proviso should come as no surprise to those involved with GTM, since the method itself grew from precisely these motivations.

The metaphor of a family also evokes images of parentage and subsequent generations. The earliest GTM texts, *Awareness, Discovery,* and *Time,* (Glaser & Strauss, 1965b, 1967, 1968) must be seen as products of various influences and strands of thought and practice brought together through the work of three progenitors: Barney Glaser, Anselm Strauss, and Jeanne Quint (later Jeanne Quint Benoliel). The contrasting backgrounds of Strauss and Glaser are now fairly well understood, although differing views have been expressed regarding the impact and influence these formations had on GTM itself. (See Charmaz, 2014a; Gibson & Hartman, 2014; and below.)

The role of Quint, on the other hand, has only recently become more widely acknowledged when GTM is discussed. Although her brilliant article, 'Institutionalized practices of information control' (Quint, 1965), confirmed her analytic skill, her earliest contributions to the method remain less visible. Quint learned field research from Anselm Strauss and worked with Strauss and Glaser on their projects on death and dying before she wrote her doctoral dissertation on identity among children with juvenile diabetes, receiving her PhD in nursing in 1969. Quint's role was critical in data collection for the death and dying project, but she seldom appears in discussions of the development of GTM.[1] She made various contributions to the literature on GTM and qualitative methods in nursing research throughout her career (see, for example, Benoliel, 1984, 1996).[2]

More controversially, Phyllis Stern (2012), in her obituary for Quint, argued that '[W]hen Glaser and Strauss *treated her data as their own*, she beat them to the punch by publishing first' (emphasis added). The book in question was *The Nurse and the Dying Patient* (Quint, 1967). Kathy Charmaz, contributing much of the detail here about Quint, has pointed out that her book actually used some of Glaser and Strauss's substantive concepts, published in earlier papers.

Quint's book, appearing in 1967, offered a thorough description of what student nurses learned about working with dying patients, and their attitudes and actions towards them. The book contributed to monumental changes in the care of the dying, but was neither a methodological exegesis nor a grounded theory.

Given the important turn in GTM research, and research generally, to question the position from which research is carried out (see below), it is important that Quint's critical if circumscribed role is acknowledged and understood. For instance, one of the earliest papers resulting from this research appeared in 1964 with the names of all three authors in the following order – Strauss, Glaser, and Quint (1964).

Looking back after 50 years, it might be hard to grasp the impact that Glaser and Strauss's writings had on US social science. If researchers in the 1960s did not realize it before, then *Discovery* made it clear that there was a dominant, if largely taken-for-granted and unexamined, mode of *doing* social science research in the USA. As Adele Clarke points out in her chapter (CD:1), Glaser and Strauss's impact on conventional conceptions and practices of research cannot be overstated. These conventions encompassed methodological-cum-procedural aspects, but also institutional-cum-hierarchical ones. All neatly evoked by Glaser and Strauss's imagery of 'theoretical capitalists and proletarian researchers', the latter toiling hypothetico-deductively amid the minutiae of the most notable theorists – particularly the Parsonians and Mertonians: i.e. Talcott Parsons and R. K. Merton. *Discovery* (1967), together with the two paradigm examples of GTM-in-use – *Awareness of Dying* (1965b) and *Time for Dying* (1968) – offered new insights into existing research practices as well as a new way of doing research, particularly at doctoral level. Although at first this was only apparent to the fortunate few enrolled on the doctoral program at the University of California San Francisco (UCSF), and to some of Glaser and Strauss's peers, who read and grasped the importance of *Discovery*. The wider impact of GTM took some time to develop, led initially by Strauss and the earliest generation of UCSF doctoral graduates. (NB: Not every sociologist agreed that grounded theory was new. For some Chicago school ethnographers, grounded theory restated strategies such as induction and comparative analysis, among other ideas that were common in that group.)

Discovery gained a wider readership among graduate students and researchers who wanted to do qualitative studies. In the early years following its publication, both students and established scholars relied on the book more for legitimating inductive qualitative research than for providing an explicit guide through the research process. Strauss's 1987 book, *Qualitative Analysis for Social Scientists*, and Strauss and Corbin's (1990 & 1998) *Basics of Qualitative Research* made grounded theory world-renowned. Clarke points out that the popularity of grounded theory derived from its thoroughly *empirical* orientation. She places the appeal and development of grounded theory in its historical context. Most sociological research at the time was theory-driven. Clarke explicitly addresses the abductive, iterative movement between empirical materials and theory as part of the method from its early beginnings. Although few researchers wrote about abduction, it had always been part of the method for those who studied with Strauss.

Kathy Charmaz debated whether to include a section on abduction in an early paper (1983) but decided against it because the paper introduced grounded theory to students and was intended to clarify a method that few researchers of the day understood. I now argue (Bryant, 2017) that abduction, or our understanding of it, has come of age and is a vital part of research discussions. Several chapters in both *Handbooks* (Bryant & Charmaz, 2007a, 2019) provide vital discussions on abduction.

Discovery proposed an alternative to classical hypothetico-deductive research, where theoretical issues and hypotheses were derived from existing 'authoritative' work, and then subjected to 'verification' in the field. Instead, it was argued that researchers should immerse themselves in their chosen research context from the start, and allow theories to 'emerge' from the data. I would argue that this metaphor was often taken too far, even by Glaser and Strauss themselves (see below), who suggested that researchers could and should abandon their previous theoretical knowledge and experience before analyzing their data.

Glaser and Strauss, however, recognized that this naïve inductivism was unrealistic and unworkable, arguing that researchers needed to develop their 'theoretical sensitivity'; the ability to conceptualize relevant data in theoretical terms, which can be only achieved by drawing on already existing theories and models. Kelle (CD:3) argues that

> [T]he development of Grounded Theory Methodology (GTM) was characterized by different attempts to elaborate the concept of 'theoretical sensitivity' and to describe modes of a non-deductive use of theories and models in the process of empirically grounded theory building. Thereby a variety of new and complex concepts were proposed like 'theoretical coding', 'coding families', 'axial coding', 'coding paradigm', and many others.

It might be an exaggeration to ask 'who now reads Talcott Parsons and/or Robert Merton?',[3] but it is certainly the case that, at least from the 1990s onwards, far more researchers and students across many disciplines read, cite, and use Glaser and Strauss – both individually and in concert – than do likewise for Parsons or Merton.[4]

A focus on methods has developed since the 1960s, itself in part an effect of the publication of *Discovery*. From my experience as a doctoral student in social science in the UK in the 1970s, the issue of 'methods' was not a priority; there were few, if any, support sessions on the topic, and very few texts particularly on qualitative methods. The situation in the USA, where doctoral programs – such as that at UCSF – included taught qualitative methods courses and epistemological assessments, was markedly different. In the interim, and with apologies to Jane Austen, it is now a truth universally acknowledged that a research student in pursuit of a doctorate must be in want of a clear and extended account of their research design and method(s).[5]

At least since the 1990s, a standard expectation is that all research reports devote a specific section to research methods, and researchers are expected to justify their research strategy, either planned (for research proposals) or carried out in arriving at the results of the study in question. This expectation is a welcome development since it ensures that research findings are not reported in some mysterious or furtive manner. Rather, the overall process, including the trade-offs and decisions endemic to research, is rendered visible and accountable. One downside occurs if such discussions are untruthful or retro-fitted to the findings: what might be termed *methodological hindsight*. Unfortunately, GTM, when deliberately or unwittingly misunderstood and misrepresented, has proved particularly 'convenient' in these instances. This has led to credibility issues when assessors and other 'gate-keepers' are confronted with GTM research proposals or outputs, often with at best only a tenuous connection to the method itself.

Mis-application of methods, however, is not confined to GTM or qualitative methods, and some degree of methodological scepticism is essential for anyone evaluating research proposals or outputs. GTM suffers disproportionately in this regard because it appears, erroneously, to offer a *laissez-faire* or 'anything goes' model of research. Also, since it is far-and-away the most widely used method in many domains, there are far more examples of good, bad, and indifferent GTM-oriented research than any other. Writers on GTM need to take account of both issues – they are two sides of the same coin: the flexibility and open-mindedness inherent in GTM affords researchers the basis for investigative strategies that can lead to novel insights and innovative outcomes. As a consequence, the method has widespread appeal to early-career researchers and others looking for ways in which they can move beyond the confines of specific disciplines or customary or 'expected' modes of investigation. The downside of such popularity and widespread appeal is that, in some cases, invoking GTM amounts to little more than a methodological veneer, disguising inadequate attention to research design. This observation is certainly not restricted to GTM, but it is compounded by its popularity, since there are so many more research papers and other outputs than is the case for other methods. There is, consequently, more scope for ambiguities and misunderstandings in statements regarding GTM, particularly since advocates of different variants do not always couch their arguments in the clearest and most respectful manner. Judith Holton (CD:20) quotes Nagel et al. (2015), who note that novice GTM researchers have to weave their way

> through a myriad of paths in a landscape of varied and divergent perspectives ... differences of opinion ... differing paradigmatic inclinations or lack of agreement amongst established GT methods and procedures (p. 366) ... [this confusion is compounded by the] ... lack of respect for alternate approaches within [the] GT community, terminology varied and fluid, slurring of methods between approaches (p. 369).

It must be noted, however, that the phrase 'fluid, slurring of methods' is used here in a pejorative manner, which is unfortunate and unwelcome since it is important to respect alternative methodological positions, and to encourage and foster *methodological sensitivity* as part of research practice – see Rapoport's rules below.

In too many cases, however, those assessing and evaluating research proposals and publications appear to have little or no familiarity with GTM. Often their assessments exhibit various prejudices that preclude clear and cogent assessment and evaluation. Given that GTM has been in use for more than 50 years, this is a severe failing on the part of academic gate-keepers. There is now, however, a growing recognition of this issue, with some GTM writers presenting guidelines to assist gate-keepers in their deliberations, and advice for those submitting their work to pre-empt what I have termed 'a strange hostility' to GTM. For instance, the summary tables in my recent book (Bryant, 2017, Chapter 18) aimed specifically at research students, GTM-researchers, research assessors, PhD examiners, journal editors, and reviewers.

Rapoport's four rules

The period immediately following publication of *Discovery* witnessed a gradual advance in knowledge, use, and teaching of GTM as graduates from the doctoral program at UCSF moved out into the academic field, both in the USA and elsewhere – particularly in Germany. But it was only in the 1990s that its influence grew by several orders of magnitude, largely through publication of Strauss's (1987) work, and his subsequent work with Juliet Corbin (Strauss & Corbin, 1990 & 1998). Since then GTM has developed, resulting in several variants of the method (see below), and it behoves all those writing about GTM to ensure that they offer clear and balanced accounts of these alternatives.

If one's position is largely derived from one specific perspective, this should be made clear, with respectful attention drawn to the ways in which other accounts differ, ensuring that any rebuttal or criticism only takes place after the opposing position has been expressed clearly and accurately, together with key points that are common to both and anything that has been learned from the differing view.

This proviso is a critical concern, and all those writing about and teaching GTM need to consider the impact their critical comments may have on those seeking clarification and guidance. I deliberately opened my recent book on GTM quoting Rapoport's four rules regarding how to write a successful critical commentary on someone's work. They are worth quoting in full.

1. First, he said, you must attempt to re-express your opponent's position so clearly, vividly, and fairly that your opponent says 'Thanks, I wish I'd thought of putting it that way'.
2. Then, you should list any points of agreement (especially if they are not matters of general or widespread agreement).
3. Third, you should mention anything you have learned from your opponent.
4. Only then are you permitted to say so much as a word of rebuttal or criticism. (Bryant, 2017, p. ix)

I have sought to ensure that this monograph adheres to these precepts, albeit that I take issue with various writers, including some of those who have contributed to *Current Developments* (Bryant & Charmaz, 2019). I offer my apologies to anyone who feels poorly treated in this extended discussion, but trust that any differences can be discussed if not resolved in a fruitful and respectful manner.

After *Discovery* – first and second generations and beyond

Writing in the early 1990s, 25 years after *Discovery*, Strauss and Corbin observed that

> … no inventor has permanent possession of the invention – certainly not even its name – and furthermore we would not wish to do so. No doubt we will always prefer the later versions of grounded theory that are closest to or elaborate our own, but a child once launched is very much subject to a combination of its origins and the evolving contingencies of life. Can it be otherwise with a methodology? (Strauss & Corbin, 1994, p. 283)

Twenty-five years later, and given the popularity of the method, it is not surprising that there has been a burgeoning of texts and other resources on the method itself, together with an enormous number of completed PhDs and larger research projects across a growing number of disciplines. Glaser has continued to publish his own texts as well as establishing and encouraging initiatives such as *The Grounded Theory Institute*,[6] which offers support and visibility to GTM researchers, including doctoral students. Juliet Corbin has published two further editions of *Basics of Qualitative Research* (Corbin & Strauss, 2008 & 2015), while Kathy Charmaz has produced a second edition of *Constructing Grounded Theory* (2014a, 3rd edition in preparation), as well as significant writings that address issues of social justice from a GTM perspective. I have published *Grounded Theory and Grounded Theorizing* (Bryant, 2017), drawing on the work of many of my PhD students over the years, and explicitly addressing the Pragmatist orientation in the method. Other developments in the method can be found in the work of Clarke's *Situational Analysis* (2005, 2015; Clarke et al., 2017), and Morse et al. (2009 & 2016) have addressed the ways in which GTM has moved on to a second generation, offering an account of GTM that includes contributions from six key grounded theorists who all worked with and/or studied under Strauss.

These works, in many cases authored by contributors to the two *Handbooks*, have developed and enhanced GTM since the 1990s, when Strauss and Corbin made their point about the 'evolving contingencies'. These variations and developments can be bewildering to those with little or no familiarity with GTM, but they are testimony to the vitality and importance of the method. It would be a far more serious indictment if GTM had failed to produce new variants and off-shoots since *Discovery*.

Strauss, Glaser, and Quint-Benoliel comprise the first generation of grounded theorists; Morse et al. are key figures from the second generation (see Morse et al., 2009 & 2016), together with their 'cousins' in the German-speaking tradition. The situation now is significantly more complex and diverse, with several variants, leading to a situation where it is important to distinguish between the 'essences' and the 'accidents' of GTM (see Bryant, 2017, Chapter 4). Katja Mruck and Günter Mey (CD:23) argue that one can characterize GTM approaches in terms of generation, background, and epistemology. Joanna Crossman and Hiroko Noma (CD:29) note that Charmaz 'has argued that the cultural, economic, historical, political and geographic conditions of the United States have determined the logic, values, epistemological assumptions and worldview that influence the kinds of problems investigated and the research questions posed within grounded theory', and has also contended that the grounded theory method itself reflects the economic, social, and historical conditions in the US in the early 1960s.

Crossman and Noma go on to argue that it is ironic that 'few scholars have explored the cultural assumptions that underpin the methodology itself', given that GTM incorporates a call to study phenomena *in situ*. They see this as part of a wider strategy to investigate 'the implications of globalization and more specifically, internationalization, for the teaching, learning, practice and development of grounded theory'. They also refer to Ralph, Birks, and Chapman (2015), who

> argue that a contemporaneous interpretation of grounded theory is dependent upon prevailing forces that shape societal views about the world and ultimately, the ontological and epistemological assumptions of the researcher. Over time, changing circumstances and the responsiveness of grounded theorists to them, affect methodological consumerism, or more specifically, the extent to which communities become receptive to variants of grounded theory.

These early statements were further developed as part of the doctoral program at UCSF. Given that this group of researchers and the first generation of students included Anselm Strauss, Barney Glaser, Virginia Olesen, Patrick Biernacki, Kathy Charmaz, Phyllis Stern, Carolyn Wiener, Juliet Corbin, and Adele Clarke, among others, it is not surprising that a rich variety of articulations and examples of the method-in-use arose in this period. Taken together, they attest to the vibrancy and vitality that the method engendered among a talented and articulate subgroup within the larger research community. *Discovery* itself had enormous impact on new scholars, who embraced it as justification for conducting inductive qualitative research. A paucity of such developments would have indicated that Glaser and Strauss's manifesto had fallen on deaf ears or was ill-founded and unworthy of further consideration.[7]

Grounded theory before *Discovery*

It is important to stress the originality of GTM, but its precursors must also be recognized, albeit discussing them in no way diminishes the pioneering work of Strauss, Glaser, and Quint. We need to understand how earlier work was influential and, in some cases, re-fashioned and incorporated into GTM. This, together with re-evaluation of the importance of Quint's role, amounts to a re-discovery or re-construction of the history and development of GTM.

One feature of this has been the increasing attention paid to studies with which Strauss was involved before he teamed up with Glaser (see Flick, CD:6). For example, in *Awareness* (1965b) reference is made to the pioneering study of medical training, *Boys in White* (Becker et al., 1961), with a footnote on page 4 referring to the realization that the standard training of medical students failed to address the issue of how to interact with dying patients and their relatives. (For younger readers, in those unenlightened times boys became doctors, girls were, for the most part, channelled into nursing.) This realization was 'the result of a secondary analysis of field-notes from a study of Kansas Medical School published as *Boys in White*' (Becker et al., 1961). Other examples include *Psychiatric Ideologies and Institutions* (Strauss, 1964), and 'The hospital and its negotiated order' (Strauss et al., 1963).

Strauss's background as a leading exponent of the 'Chicago School of Sociology' was key to his development, and that of GTM. Many writers have commented on this, but rarely go further in their analysis. Alvin Gouldner (1973), a colleague of Strauss, writing in the 1970s, made some important observations regarding Strauss's intellectual formation. Strauss is listed together with Howard Becker and Erving Goffman as exemplifying 'the purest vein of Romanticism[8] in American sociology'. For Gouldner, Romanticism embodied a trend in thought that rebelled against 'disciplined conformity to ... received and impersonal rules' (1973, p. 327). Initially this stance was purely dogmatic, lacking any 'rationale of a new language or a new logic'. Gouldner traces this trend through the development of European social thought, noting that the Romantics and the Positivists shared an antipathy towards traditional forms of authority. The former seeking a new basis in the imagination, and the latter in science. Seeing a congruence between Romanticism and Positivism is highly unusual, but Gouldner's argument is noteworthy and persuasive.

Having postulated this link between 'imagination' (Romanticism) and 'science' (Positivism), Gouldner characterizes GTM, through Strauss, as seeking to combine the strengths of both. He argues that

Strauss (together with B. Glaser) [who] has spoken for the merits of 'data-grounded theory' [*sic!*] [the method being] primarily a polemic against deductive, formal styles of sociological theorizing and an argument for inductive theorizing – once again revealing the paradoxical but abiding affinity of certain forms of Positivism and Romanticism. (Gouldner, 1973, p. 345, see online version)

Gouldner quotes Strauss describing Romanticism in the hands of G. H. Mead, who stripped it of its 'mysticism' and gave it 'biological and scientific traits', providing the basis for prying open 'the deterministic framework of modern science' restating 'problems of autonomy, freedom and innovation' (1973, p. 348).

Here is an intimation of the tension in early GTM, between imagination on the one hand, and a positivist view of science on the other, also drawing attention to the Pragmatist and emancipatory predispositions in GTM that are now more widely understood. All built upon Glaser and Strauss's concern to delegitimize the existing hierarchy in US social science. Charmaz's (2000) delineation between 'objectivist' and 'constructivist' forms of GTM can be seen as a restatement and enhancement of Gouldner's earlier analysis, but her demarcation necessarily places greater emphasis on the imaginative aspects in the light of the critiques of 'normal science', positivism, and 'scientism' that have gained ground and significance since the 1960s. The incorporation of 'imagination' into social theorizing opens the way for abduction, integrating Peirce (1986, 1992) and Mead (1934, 1959 [1932]), and the Pragmatism of Dewey (1929, 1938) and James (2000), with GTM (see below).

There are then strong ties between Chicago School sociology and GTM. But GTM also encompasses Glaser's contribution, and through him, aspects of the social theorizing from Columbia University in New York in the immediate post-war period. Again, Gouldner offers useful insights, referring to Paul Lazarsfeld, a key influence on Glaser. For Gouldner in the 1970s, Lazarsfeld was 'surely the dean of social science methodologists in the United States today', yet his (Lazarsfeld's) position was that social scientists should not be guided first and foremost by 'formal canons of science' but by 'the *implicit* rules and procedures which successful social scientists *tacitly* employ and embody in their researches' (Gouldner, 1973, p. 355, emphasis in original). Gouldner argues that Lazarsfeld viewed social science research proceeding 'on the basis of (at first) *inarticulate* operational rules and often *ineffable* information or experience' (emphasis added). The 'inarticulateness of the creative ... needs to be rendered articulate'. Gouldner concludes that while the 'sociological *theorists* at Chicago University were more Romantic that those at Columbia University, it may be that the statistical *methodologists* at Columbia University were more Romantic than those elsewhere' (p. 356). Gouldner effectively provides an outline lineage for GTM: Romanticism reinterpreted by Mead, drawing on John Dewey and Pragmatism, combined with a *methodological* view of creativity via Lazarsfeld.

It is crucial, however, to understand that, while making these associations, I am not arguing that such precursors explain, anticipate, or devalue the innovations of GTM. On the contrary, in many respects Strauss and Glaser specifically turned against or re-invented key aspects of their respective intellectual influences. Strauss certainly built on the work of Mead and other Chicago sociologists, often re-orienting or revising some key aspects. For instance, as Jörg Strübing argues (CD:2):

> In shifting the Blumerian emphasis from *symbolic* interaction towards a more material view of sociality as situated activity, and thereby blurring the somewhat artificial separation of action from structure, Strauss both established a strictly anti-dualistic view of the social and showed the dynamic tension between doubt and belief to be the mover of human activity.

Re-constructing the history of GTM: Archaeology and genealogy

This trend of re-invention or enhancement has continued as GTM has developed, producing a rich diversity. Thus, Strübing contends that Strauss retained and strengthened the link to Pragmatism that Blumer had undone; but it is only in more recent times that this link and its ramifications for GTM have been discussed and articulated.

In similar vein, Gregory Hadley (CD:28) points out that Theodor Adorno denounced Lazarsfeld's preference for simply describing life as it is, without also suggesting how it *should* be, resulting in 'a bourgeois sociology reinforcing the domination inherent in society' (quoting Gibson, 2007, p. 438).[9] Hadley notes that similar criticism was raised against Symbolic Interactionism, and later directed at GTM itself by Layder (1993) and Burawoy (1991), who argued that Grounded Theorists, claiming to let the data speak for itself, are merely supporting the status quo. Hadely quotes Kincheloe and McLaren (2000) who explain that theoretical descriptions 'are not simply about the world but serve to construct it ... language in the form of discourses serves as a form of regulation and domination (2000, p. 284)'. The recent work relating GTM to issues around social justice and inequality can then be understood as consciously remedying this omission or inattention in earlier grounded theories. Charmaz has led the way in attending to these concerns, and, contrary to the sorts of criticism of Layder and Burawoy, argues that GTM, through its lineage with Symbolic Interaction and Pragmatism, inherently encompasses issues of social justice and critical inquiry, a theme developed by Duckles et al. (CD:31), explicitly taking their lead from recent work by Charmaz (2017a).

Taken together this provides the basis for a genealogy for GTM, understood in Nietzsche's philosophical sense, later developed by Foucault. Genealogy is not the investigation of a glorious past culminating in the present, but rather something that is complex, mundane, and contingent. The *Stanford Encyclopedia of Philosophy* (SEP) refers to this as follows:

> Foucault intended the term 'genealogy' to evoke Nietzsche's genealogy of morals, particularly with its suggestion of complex, mundane, inglorious origins – in no way part of any grand scheme of progressive history. The point of a genealogical analysis is to show that a given system of thought (itself uncovered in its essential structures by archaeology, which therefore remains part of Foucault's historiography) was the result of contingent turns of history, not the outcome of rationally inevitable trends. (*Stanford Encyclopedia of Philosophy*, n.d. – entry on genealogy)

Several chapters in both *Handbooks* (Bryant & Charmaz, 2007a & 2019) offer accounts of how GTM developed, and, in many instances, they extend its history to the period before publication of *Awareness* and *Discovery*. These accounts amount to an archaeology of GTM in Foucault's sense, with different archaeologists coming up with differing accounts, albeit with extensive areas of agreement and mutual support. In so doing, the genealogy of GTM is further clarified. Gouldner offers an early example; later ones focus on what we now understand to be key issues for GTM – e.g. the role and nature of what was meant by 'induction' in the early works, the influence of Pragmatism, the relationship to Symbolic Interaction, and the contingencies that brought Quint, Strauss, and Glaser together at UCSF.

This all contributes to a 're-construction' of the history of GTM, with the proviso that all histories are understood to be constructions in one way or another (see Bryant et al., 2013; Maines et al., 1983; Mead, 1959 [1932]).

Critically this re-construction needs to incorporate the ways in which our current understanding of GTM differs from people's understanding at the time of its first articulation, and at various points in the 50+ years since its appearance. We can all benefit from engaging in a dialogue with those earlier statements, building upon them and adding new insights. Inevitably this will involve some challenges to the 'received wisdom', just as Glaser and Strauss's original work challenged the orthodoxy of the 1960s.

Once we move beyond the work of Quint, Glaser, and Strauss in the 1960s things get more complex. The initial corpus of work and teaching of the method was located at UCSF, although not all those in the initial cohort of the PhD programme completed PhDs using GTM, and of those who did, only a few later undertook GTM-oriented research. Quint went on to build upon the work on dying, incorporating it into professional nursing practices and helping to establish what we now understand as terminal/hospice care. Glaser's role at UCSF was confined to teaching the grounded theory seminars.[10] He also produced his key text *Theoretical Sensitivity* (1978) in this period. Only in the 1990s did he take on a higher GTM profile, including publishing, teaching, and mentoring – activities with which he continues to be deeply involved.

Strauss was the key promulgator of GTM in the 1970s and 1980s, lecturing and publishing widely. He ran several GTM studies with former doctoral students (e.g. Fagerhaugh, Suczek, and Weiner), and worked with Juliet Corbin in 1980 when she was a doctoral student in nursing. She collaborated with Strauss until his death in 1996. Corbin and Strauss published widely during the 1980s, including *Unending Work and Care: Managing Chronic Illness at Home* (1988). Their collaboration led to publication of *Basics of Qualitative Research* in 1990. At the same time, the German-speaking GTM tradition was flourishing – see below.

Together with mention of Quint's contribution, the ways in which the work of Strauss and his colleagues in Chicago can be seen as nascent GTM studies has been noted, although this is in no way to disparage or minimize Glaser's contribution. Identifying the antecedents is at best a case of establishing the necessary but not sufficient conditions for the development of GTM. On the other hand, in some of his recent writings, Glaser seems to be offering his own re-construction of the history of GTM. In an article that first appeared in *The Grounded Theory Review* in 2014, he wrote as follows:

> In this book I am writing about only the application of classic GT *as I originated it in 1967* in which the concepts of a GT theory are abstract of time, place, and people. (Glaser, 2014, emphasis added)

It may be that this is overstatement rather than a claim to be the sole originator of the method, but as it stands it is highly misleading.

One key statement re-constructing the history of GTM is the article by Strauss and Corbin in the first edition of *The Handbook of Qualitative Research* in 1994. The authors noted that it had taken more than 20 years for the US sociological establishment to appreciate the 'strong rationale' for qualitative research lying at the core of GTM from its earliest embodiments. For Strauss and Corbin there was the danger – in the mid-1990s – that GTM would become fashionable and 'would later be seen as old-hat'.

GTM in Germany[11]

Strauss held many visiting posts in Europe from the mid-1950s onwards, but his first visit to Germany in the aftermath of publication of *Discovery* was in 1975, when he was invited, by Thomas Luckmann, to spend time at the University of Konstanz as a researcher. There he met, among others, Hans Georg Soeffner. Soeffner spent time with Strauss at UCSF in the late 1980s and early 1990s, collaborating with Strauss and colleagues, including Jeff Froner, Susan Leigh Star, and Adele Clarke, on a research project about 'illegals' in the Bay Area.

In the late 1970s Fritz Schütze visited Strauss in San Francisco; so too did Gerd Riemann (University of Kassel), Richard Grathoff (Bielefeld) and Bruno Hildenbrand (Konstanz). Udo Kelle (personal communication) notes, however, that at this time 'Glaser and Strauss were more widely known among medical sociologists for their work on interaction with dying patients than for their methodological writings'. Hence one of the earliest references to Glaser and Strauss's work in Germany appears in the paper by Uta Gerhardt in 1976 'Krankenkarriere und Existenzbelastung' ('Healthcare and the burden of existence').

Kelle also notes that the initial dissemination of Glaser and Strauss's methodological work, in 1979, was the German translation of their 1965 paper 'Discovery of substantive theory: A basic strategy underlying qualitative research', originally published in *American Behavioural*

Scientist (Glaser & Strauss, 1965a). The translation appeared in *Qualitative Sozialforschung*, edited by Christel Hopf and Elmar Weingarten, with the title 'Die Entdeckung gegenstandsbezogener Theorie'. Kelle points out that throughout the 1980s and the early 1990s GTM was referred to in Germany as '*gegenstandsbezogene Theoriebildung* or *gegenstandsnahe Theoriebildung* (the original German translation for "substantive theory" building)'.

In 1982 Soeffner, Grathoff, and Schütze invited Strauss to Germany for a study visit, where he met Jo Reichertz. During this visit he produced

> a Study Letter for the students of sociology of the FernUniversität Hagen with the title: Qualitative analysis in social research: Grounded theory methodology: Study Letter, University Hagen. It was an early version of *Qualitative Analysis for Social Scientists* (Strauss, 1987). For some years I used to be the tutor of this course. (Reichertz, personal communication)

A German translation of Strauss's 1987 book appeared in 1991, edited by Hildenbrand, and a German edition of Strauss and Corbin's book followed in 1996. But as Strübing points out, Strauss's work was already well known in Germany, based on the 1968 translation of 'his early masterpiece' *Mirrors and Masks* (Strauss, 1959). Among German sociologists *Spiegel und Masken* was the key text for understanding issues of identity and interaction, ahead of Goffman's work *Presentation of Self in Everyday Life* (1959).

Constructing grounded theories – GTM as a method-in-use

One aspect of the history of GTM that is critically unarticulated is the way in which the progenitors worked. The early GTM research projects involved all three, and *Awareness*, *Discovery*, and *Time* were produced collaboratively by Glaser and Strauss (1965b, 1967, 1968). Yet they never offered any extensive discussion of how this collaboration developed and operated. A brief hint appears in *Status Passage*, their only jointly produced formal grounded theory. Describing their method for 'Generating Formal Theory' (Glaser & Strauss, 1971, Chapter 9, pp. 192–193), they note that:

Because so much relevant data and theory was 'in us' from our previous work, the principal mode used to generate theory was to talk out our comparisons in lengthy conversations, and either *record the conversation or take notes.* We ... studied relevant literature for more data and theory. These conversations went on almost five days a week for three months. At this time we gave up in exhaustion, and with the realization that we could begin to write it all up. (emphasis added)

It would be interesting to know more about their working practices. Strauss's earlier experiences and observations, and later his six months of preliminary fieldwork, shaped the initial analysis of the social organization of death and dying (see Glaser & Strauss, 1965b, pp. 286–287). Glaser joined the project five months after it received funding, and they soon worked out concepts concerning death-expectations and awareness. The data relied on observations and interviews, and perhaps other resources, although it is not clear how much of the data collection they did themselves. Moreover, there is little indication of how they worked on the data. They seem to have recorded their discussions in developing *Status Passage,* so did they do likewise in developing *Awareness* and *Time*; if so, did this involve only the two of them? How did they analyze their data? Did they each code the same data separately and then meet to discuss their individual findings, or did they work things out together from scratch? What happened if they differed in their analyses? Do their field-notes or memos survive in any form?

In the 2007 volume, the chapter by Carolyn Wiener (2007) focused specifically on team-working, offering an account of how some of the early doctoral graduates at UCSF worked with Strauss on several major projects. Her account gives a glimpse of how Strauss worked with others, both academic colleagues and former doctoral students.

Accounts and insights into how research is actually carried out are few-and-far-between, which is unfortunate since it gives free rein to the stereotype of the lone, usually male, researcher, reinforced in films, books, plays, awards of international prizes, and so on. Early-career researchers, and PhD students in particular, often feel isolated and in need of guidance, not only from experienced advisors and supervisors, but also from those who are only a few steps ahead of them in their development. In recent years, students' accounts have appeared (e.g. Bryant, 2017, Chapter 19), and various forms of research workshop provide a forum for such interactions. Yet it is ironic and unfortunate that the process of researching in all its various forms is itself so under-researched. In particular, wider recognition and understanding of the ways in which researchers work together need to be developed, undermining the mistaken assumption that research is for the most part a one-*man* [*sic*] endeavour.

For GTM specifically, there is the issue of the role of the supervisor/advisor at various stages of doctoral research. Glaser has made continuous use of Phyllis Stern's term 'minus mentoring', i.e. where PhD students, aiming to use GTM, are supervised by staff with little or no understanding of the method, or, even worse, a highly imperfect and ill-informed one. This applies across all methods, but with regard to GTM it seems to be particularly problematic. I am aware of cases where students have been told erroneously that (a) they cannot use GTM as 'they have already read the literature', (b) they need clear research questions and hypotheses at the start of their research, (c) that their coding is 'incorrect', and that their advisor has a 'better understanding' of the data.

One problem with the term 'discovery', coupled with an often unstated but influential objectivist epistemology, is that it can lead to a view that the grounded theory resulting from use of GTM in a research project could indeed have been discovered by any researcher with the requisite skills. Thus, an advisor assisting, guiding or even correcting a doctoral student in their coding might be thought to be acting legitimately and helpfully since the codes, concepts, and theory are already embryonically in the data.

As Gouldner noted in 1973, GTM is at least as much about 'imagination' and creativity as it is about 'science'. This tension between 'discovery' and 'creativity' is a generic one. Charles Darwin is credited with the discovery of evolution via natural selection, but it is now understood that Alfred Russel Wallace was an independent co-discoverer. Yet if neither Darwin nor Wallace had completed and published their research, someone else would have arrived at these conclusions. Similarly, Einstein is credited with discovering relativity, but had he not done so, others would have, based on the earlier and highly regarded work of Lorentz and other theoretical physicists. Contrast this with Mozart's music or Shakespeare's plays; if neither had produced their various works, no one else would or could have done so. Grounded theories are a balanced combination of 'imagination' and 'science'. They should offer new and useful insights, the outcome of creative imaginings, albeit ones produced rigorously and transparently – abductively.

Consequently, any research mentor should refrain from active engagement with GTM-researchers, *over-mentoring*, as they develop their codes and later analysis, simultaneously ensuring that those being mentored are aware of the intricacies of employing specific methods, and the need for all researchers to develop and constantly enhance their *methodological sensitivity* (see below).

From a constructivist/interpretivist perspective, GTM-oriented research is a continuing and developing dialogue between researchers and the data. For doctoral and other early-career researchers, this dialogue also involves others, such as advisors, a term that encompasses 'promoters', 'Directors of Studies', and 'supervisors'. But these exchanges need to avoid both minus mentoring and over-mentoring. Recognition that GTM, or more correctly *grounded theorizing*, demands this balance leads to the understanding that conceptualizing is a skill that has to be learned, and can only be accomplished through extensive practice and trial-and-error. The dialogue then includes mentors, but their role is to facilitate the dialogue, and not intervene as a (full) participant in their mentee's work. Crossman and Noma (CD:29) focus on key aspects of mentoring. In particular, they point to the need to research into the ways in which 'students of grounded theory navigate the tricky spaces of their research'. Some are able to 'learn their craft ... in mentored relationships with other qualitative researchers and in the best of circumstances, seasoned grounded theorists'. But what can be done to assist those not so fortunate?

GTM and the interpretative turn

GTM appeared in the 1960s, coinciding with the interpretative turn, although it was only with Charmaz's writing in the 1990s that the two were brought together in any coherent, persuasive, and systematic manner. Clarke (CD:1) describes this orientation as follows:

- Meaning is re-located from 'reality out there' to 'reality as experienced by the perceiver';
- An observer is assumed to inevitably be a *participant* in what is observed, more or less reflexive;
- Interpretations are not universal but must be located and situated in space and time;
- Cultures are best understood as unevenly changing assemblages of distinctive symbols and signifying practices;
- Interpretation *per se* is conditioned by historic cultural perspectives and mediated by symbols and practices.

In essence, using Rorty's (1999) succinct paraphrase, for interpretivism/ constructivism truth is *made*, whereas for positivists or objectivists truth is *discovered*. Glaser and Strauss's *Discovery* can now be seen perhaps as an unfortunate misnomer, albeit that the title confronted the orthodoxy of the time: 'discovery' implying that the 'proletarian researchers' could and should develop their own concepts, challenging the 'theoretical capitalists' in their academic redoubts. In contrast, by the 1990s Charmaz was developing and articulating the constructivist view of GTM, culminating in *Constructing Grounded Theory* (2006), which can be seen as a cogent and genuinely innovative re-statement of the method, fully engaged with and incorporating the interpretative turn.

There were, however, premonitions of this even in the 1960s. Leonard Schatzman, who worked with Strauss in Chicago and at UCSF, was responsible for the UCSF course on field methods. Students took this in preparation for the GTM courses taught first by Glaser and later by Strauss. Schatzman interacted with the teachers and students at UCSF for many years, continuing the tradition of the Chicago School, offering students the opportunity to discuss their work from its earliest stages with their peers and others.

Jane Gilgun quotes Marianne McCarthy, who participated in a group independent study with Schatzman: 'The group independent study was wonderful. ... We worked as a group, critiqued each others' fieldnotes and each others' memos' (Gilgun, 1993). Schatzman's method of Dimensional Analysis was developed in response to GTM, partly to support students who found GTM hard going. 'The method Strauss teaches and Glaser teaches is very, very difficult. ... It simply is not easy to grasp' (Gilgun, 1993). Although to an extent Schatzman's method might be seen as too prescriptive, it encouraged students to work within an interpretive perspective, developing what I have termed *methodological sensitivity*.

Methodological sensitivity can be defined as the skill or aptitude required by researchers in selecting, combining, and employing methods, techniques, and tools in actual research situations. Researchers can and need to develop this skill as a result of a combination of:

- guidance from and working with other researchers;
- insightful study of available research methods, techniques, and tools;
- and learning from their own experience. (See Bryant, 2017, Chapter 2)

Hadley (CD:28) argues that Schatzman developed Dimensional Analysis as a partial form of GTM, but one that 'nevertheless anticipated the next turn that took place in GT, which was to understand social reality as more elastic', partly anticipating Charmaz's constructivist form. Kearney (2007, p. 129) noted that Strauss described his first large-scale research venture, *Psychiatric Ideologies and Institutions* (1964), where Schatzman was a co-author, as 'virtually a grounded theory study, but only implicitly so'.

Hadley (CD:28) echoes Gouldner in stating that this development characterizes coding as 'less a question of scientific technique and more of an intuitive art developed according to the researcher's individual talents, worldview, and temperament'. Interestingly, he sees this development taken further in Clarke's *Situational Analysis*, 'a postmodern, relativist Grounded Theory, similar to Charmaz (2006, 2014a), [that] highlights the process of *theorizing* over the product of theory' (Hadley's emphasis). Schatzman commended Glaser and Strauss for their contribution in articulating GTM, simultaneously challenging others to do likewise. 'Their great contribution was to push us into making methodological commitments which historically we did not do' (quoted in Gilgun, 1993). But he also saw how these methodological statements could solidify and so become barriers to researchers' efforts at constructing theoretical insights; i.e. being treated as algorithms rather than as heuristics (see Bryant, 2017, Chapter 2).

There are various ways of describing the different forms of GTM, and how they relate to one another. For instance, we can identify the canonical works of Glaser and Strauss in the 1960s, from which three main variants have developed, exemplified by:

1. Strauss and Corbin's writings, particularly those from the 1990s;
2. Glaser's writings, particularly those from the 1990s;
3. The constructivist writings of Charmaz (2000, 2006, 2014a) and later Bryant (2002, 2017) beginning in the 1990s.

In addition, and in many cases cutting across these three forms, or intersecting with at least one of them, are approaches such as Clarke's *Situational Analysis* (2005; Clarke et al., 2017).

Jo Reichertz (CD:13), however, refers to 'at least *five* different varieties which are arranged consecutively, suggesting one may also talk about *various phases* of its development or about *different generations* of Grounded Theory'. In order these are:

1. 'Inductively oriented' GT – i.e. as evidenced in Glaser and Strauss's earliest writings in the 1960s, but also including Glaser's later writings since they maintain the stance of 'the researcher [remaining] passive ... which leads to the reasonable objection that this approach is ingrained with *Positivism*'.
2. 'Classic' GT – i.e. the work of Strauss in the 1980s, and later his earliest empirical work with Corbin: 'ingrained in American *Pragmatics* (Peirce, Dewey, Mead) ... [with] similarities to a *(non-reflective) sociology of knowledge* and to *social constructivism*'. Here Reichertz uses the term 'American Pragmatics' as a synonym for Pragmatism. He also deliberately uses the term 'classic' GT with regard to Strauss rather than Glaser, as the former was already in the early 1960s producing research that can be considered embryonic GT. Glaser now claims the term 'Classic' for his variant.
3. Prescriptive positivistic 'code-oriented' GT – found in the 1990 and 1998 editions of Strauss and Corbin's *Basics of Qualitative Research*, and the considerably more open-ended and flexible third and fourth editions (Corbin & Strauss, 2008 & 2015). Reichertz argues that '[T]his approach emphasizes precision, and strongly resembles *qualitative analysis of content*'. He argues that this 'variety of Grounded Theory may most likely be linked to QDA-software, e.g. ATLAS.ti, MAXQDA (Strauss & Corbin 1998; Corbin & Strauss 2008 and 2015 – and especially Corbin 2011)'.
4. His fourth type is '*Constructivist* grounded theory (Bryant 2002; Bryant & Charmaz 2007b, 2007c; Charmaz 2006, 2014a; Charmaz & Keller 2016), which especially criticizes the inductive approach of the former grounded theory methodology and moreover critically scrutinizes the capability of coding routines. This approach (referring to Pragmatism and the concept of abduction) considers research work as a search for patterns and best explanations in making comparisons and interpretations – and hence as a process which is always bound to a perspective and which is communicative.'
5. Finally, he identifies '*Postmodern, situative* grounded theory (Clarke 2005, 2007; Clarke & Keller 2014), which is explicitly not only concerned with people/social actors and their perspectives but also with artefacts, practices and discourses'.

Hadley (CD:28) refers to the 'diversity of practice' within GTM, which:

An autopoietic perspective of grounded theorization frames is both a structured product and an ongoing process. Metaphorically, it is similar to how two aunts might describe their nephew as 'a growing boy'. There is a boy (product) who is a structured entity, and a boy who is steadily growing (process). In like manner, Grounded Theories are constructions emerging from and supporting the process of ongoing theorization. Each form of theorization energizes the other along the lines of autopoiesis. All share the same genetic code. *The value of such diversity in the way GTM has been construed means that theorists have greater freedom in determining which procedures fit best for their paradigmatic, theoretical, and methodological perspective.* In the process, theories will be generated, constructed, deconstructed, and reconstructed within a system of dynamic intellectual activity. (emphasis added)

One result of this diversity is a bewildering plethora of acronyms, made more confusing since the same acronym is often used for different variants. For instance, CGT was widely used in the 2007 edition, and elsewhere, to refer to *Constructivist* GT, but it is also now used to refer to *Classic* GT – i.e. Glaser's variant (although Reichertz uses the same term to refer to Strauss's work in the 1980s) – and also to *Critical* GT.

Notes

1   Early in 2017 I was involved in the examination of a PhD in a UK university. The candidate was a practising nurse, working and researching in a highly reputable nursing department. The thesis was admirable in many respects, but failed to mention Quint in any way, and at the viva voce it was apparent that neither the candidate nor the supervisory team had any realization of Quint's importance. Needless to say, the mild set of revisions required for final award of the doctorate included the necessity for inclusion of a clear statement about her role.
2   The ways in which women are written out of history is now widely documented, if still not generally acknowledged. Examples include women artists (Parker & Pollock, 1981/1995) and women engineers and scientists.
3   Parsons posed the rhetorical question 'Who now reads (Herbert) Spencer?' in his book *The Structure of Social Action* (1937).
4   But see Jeffrey C. Alexander (1985), who claimed and revised functionalism in his book, *Neofunctionalism*, which gained interest among scholars specializing in sociological theory.
5   'It is a truth universally acknowledged, that a single man in possession of a good fortune, must be in want of a wife.' The opening of *Pride and Prejudice*, Jane Austen.
6   www.groundedtheory.com
7   Kathy Charmaz comments, 'The doctoral program was very small and most of its graduates did not have academic positions. Jobs were few in Sociology. In contrast, Nursing at the doctoral level was opening up and their doctoral students who were familiar with GT did get jobs.' (Personal Communication)
8   Romanticism is a somewhat vague and multifarious term. The entry in the *Stanford Encyclopedia of Philosophy* (n.d – entry on Romanticism) notes that '[D]istinguished scholars, such as Arthur Lovejoy, Northrop Frye and Isaiah Berlin, have remarked on the notorious challenges facing any attempt to define Romanticism. The English Romantic poet offered a succinct summation in *Ode on a Grecian Urn*: '"Beauty is truth, truth beauty,"—that is all//Ye know on earth, and all ye need to know'. Gouldner's use of the term is largely rhetorical, contrasting

Romanticism and Positivism with traditional, authoritative claims to knowledge and insight. (His article is discussed in Bryant, 2017, Chapter 18.)

9 The relationship between Adorno and Lazarsfeld was fraught in many respects – see D. E. Morrison, 'Kultur and culture: The case of Theodor W. Adorno and Paul F. Lazarsfeld'. *Social Research*, 45(2), Summer 1978.

10 Kathy Charmaz notes that earlier expectations for the formation of a School of Social and Behavioural Sciences at UCSF, with program expansion, never materialized. In the 1970s, Governor Ronald Reagan put sharp constraints on higher education in California, and sociology was declining nation-wide.

11 I am extremely grateful to Udo Kelle, Jo Reichertz, and Jörg Strübing for supplying the information on which this section is based.

2
THE CORE CHARACTERISTICS
OF GTM

Discussing GTM variants inevitably leads to consideration of the core characteristics of the method; I have offered some clarification of this, making the distinction between the 'accidents' and 'essences' of GTM (Bryant, 2017, Chapter 4, especially Table 4.4). The 'accidental' aspects mostly derive from the historical period within which GTM developed, so in time they should be revised, rectified, or clarified. The 'essential' ones are those that distinguish GTM from other approaches.

Not surprisingly, the authors of many of the chapters in *Current Developments* (Bryant & Charmaz, 2019) offer accounts of what they consider are the essential features of GTM. For instance, Johnson and Walsh (CD:25) refer to 'four foundational pillars [of the GT process]: all is data, emergence (of categories, relationships, theory, and research design), constant comparative analysis, and theoretical sampling'.

The 2007 *Handbook* introduced the distinction between the method and the output, using the term GTM for the former and GTs (grounded theories) for the latter. This usage has now become conventional to some extent, including use of the acronym GTM, although the term 'Grounded Theory' understandably continues to be used both with reference to the outcome and the method; the context usually clarifies the actual meaning. Strübing, however, takes issue with this distinction (email correspondence with author).

I have strong objections regarding the partial renaming of GT into GTM. In your paper you state that GT would be a 'misnomer'. That is not the case. It is actually an oxymoron that carries the meaning of both, the process of elaborating grounded theory and this (type of) theory itself. Why is that important? Because it is one of the key features of American pragmatism to resolve reified objects into the processes of their becoming. In order to avoid false dichotomies and to reveal the power and the decision making that goes into those objects. 'The published word is not the final one, but only a pause in the never-ending process of generating theory' (Glaser/ Strauss 1967: 40). Theory for Strauss is a process, the same process that you would like to rename GTM. That would be one step back from the advances social sciences inherited from Strauss.

To separate methods from theorizing would at the same time mean to support exactly that kind of instrumentalism that led into quantitative methods core mistakes: There is no method without theory and if it appears as such, it simply disguises its roots and its embeddedness. We should be wiser than them:-)

Robert Thornberg and Ciarán Dunne (CD:10) offer:

At least three reasons [that] account for why GTM is necessary: (1) the literature does not provide enough theories to cover all aspects or areas of the social life; (2) due to their lack of grounding in data, extant theories seldom fit or work, nor are relevant or sufficiently understandable to use in research which aspires to be sensitive to the empirical field and its participants (Glaser and Strauss, 1967); and (3) our reality is dynamic, continuously shaped by diverse, subjective lived experiences and innovations.

Norman Denzin (CD:22) argues that although GTM is 'not a unified framework' there is a common core. Despite the different variants,

there are commonalities: flexible guidelines for data collection (and analysis), including interviewing, archival analysis, observation, and participant observation. Most importantly, the commitment is to remain close to the world being studied.

He notes that some of these 'techniques' are common across other methods, albeit for differing purposes and with different approaches/commitments. More contentiously, he argues that the outputs from GTM are not theories, which is 'perhaps a misnomer ... a better word might be interpretation, grounded interpretation (GI)'.

Katherine Irwin (CD:18) refers to GTM as 'a negotiated method', and that it is 'exposure of a generation of researchers to theoretical and epistemological developments in the late 20th and early 21st centuries that accounts for why and how GTM is currently being used to develop theories linking structure and agency'. This observation brings GTM back to Strauss's work on precisely this inherently sociological issue, and the relationship between GTM and sociology discussed below.

GTM coding and sampling

Two aspects of GTM that continue to prove troubling both to exponents and evaluators are coding and sampling; largely due to the differences between their respective meanings in the context of GTM as opposed to more generic ideas in research as a whole.

Coding

Readers will probably be aware that the term 'coding', in the sense of coding data, predates the appearance of GTM. It is used in a generic sense in the context of research and data analysis, but in most cases will have an explicit meaning depending on the specific research method and/or technique that is being used.[1] Glaser and Strauss, however, deliberately changed the meaning of codes and coding in GTM, so for many researchers 'coding' is now first-and-foremost associated with GTM. But it can also be argued that coding has taken on a whole host of new meanings and nuances, particularly across qualitative research in general.[2] Unfortunately, in their later writings, both in concert and individually, they offered further expositions, often differing from the earlier ones. Susanne Friese (CD:14) notes that in the 1966 German edition, 'Strauss and Corbin define coding as "the process of data analysis" (p. 43). In the 2015 edition, it is defined as delineating concepts to stand for interpreted meaning (Chapter 12)'. This shift indicates the extent to which Corbin has sought to incorporate interpretative methods in her more recent work. CAQDAS examples, such as NVivo, MAXQDA, and Atlas.ti, use the term 'coding', but in different ways from that used in GTM and from each other. In some respects, CAQDAS 'coding' is a form of labelling or tagging, whereas GTM coding involves far more than this. Critics argue that many GTM research papers fail to move beyond the details of 'codes', offering little insight or coherence and simply re-labelling the data or describing some putative classification. But this is a failing on the part of the researchers themselves rather than anything inherent in the method.

Linda Belgrave and Kapriskie Seide (CD:8) point to the paucity of detail in the early GTM texts – particularly *Discovery* – regarding what was involved in GTM-type coding. In some regards this is understandable given that *Discovery* was primarily a manifesto written by Glaser and Strauss with their academic colleagues in mind (see Bryant, 2017, Chapter 3). More detailed expositions were provided in the methodological appendices in both *Awareness* and *Time*, these being the main sources of guidance on application of GTM in the early writings.

Later texts on GTM, however, have more than made up for this, but the result is often confusion as researchers try to make sense of the wide variety of explanations and terms that are used. Belgrave and Seide (CD:8) make the point that discussions on GTM coding must offer the basis for 'a starting point and some organizational scheme' for coding, based on an understanding of 'elements of coding approaches as steps in a process', but 'emphasizing that this process is not linear'.

They offer an overview of 'the major branches of the GTM family', including 'Glaserian GTM and Constructivist GTM, as well as a note on Computer Assisted Qualitative Data Analysis'. In doing so, they are concerned to offer a comparison of different approaches, but in

> a spirit of celebrating what we see as a rich garden of methodological possibilities, suited to diverse research paradigms. This is not to deny our differences, but to value our pluralism. In this, we see ourselves in tune with authors such as Phyllis Noerager Stern (2007), Adele Clarke (2009) and Frederick J. Wertz et al. (2011).

Belgrave and Seide stress 'the impossibility of separating coding from other elements of analysis, even writing' for GTM. This is correct up to a point, given that GTM is the method of *constant* comparison, an orientation that encompasses all the stages of GTM-oriented research, from initial coding to writing and presentation. But stated in their stark terms, it may mislead or deter GTM novices.

The consequence is that those tasked with writing about GTM coding are faced with a conundrum: efforts at 'clarification' may all too easily obfuscate and over-simplify the complexities of the processes involved, resulting in a mechanistic description of what is in fact a highly nuanced and subtle series of activities; but overly complicated and convoluted accounts might prove bewildering and unhelpful.

I have found that occasionally doctoral students, having gathered a fair amount of data – usually, but not only, from interviews – are then unable to commit themselves to coding, lacking the confidence to engage with this process. This is ironic, given that Glaser and Strauss were motivated to develop and teach GTM as a basis for giving doctoral researchers the confidence to develop their own theoretical concepts.

In some cases, such reticence arises from students misunderstanding the different forms of advice regarding getting started with coding – i.e. word-by-word or line-by-line or incident-by-incident. They need to heed Charmaz's advice that it is best to start by moving quickly through the data, rather than getting bogged down trying to identify the minutiae. Coding is one of those skills that can only be acquired through practice, even though it may appear to be straightforward. Inexperienced researchers need to trust themselves in the earliest stages and avoid wondering if they are developing 'the correct codes', instead looking for those that are most relevant and useful in developing further conceptualizations of the context under investigation.

Belgrave and Seide stress that 'coding is more than labeling', and that the ways in which the process is described by different authors reveals their respective epistemologies. They offer a very clear account, illustrated with specific examples, of five different approaches:

- the somewhat sparse accounts offered by Glaser and Strauss;
- Glaser's subsequent work;
- Strauss and Corbin's 'procedural approach';
- Charmaz and Bryant's constructivism; and
- Clarke's situational analysis.

They conclude that GTM is not 'a free-for-all', but a robust methodology, where it is both possible and advisable 'to draw from the works of multiple methodologists, bringing awareness of underlying assumptions, benefits and potential problems to one's specific project'.

Sampling

Researchers can only start their coding once they have identified the basis for their sample; again, a term that has specific connotations within GTM, diverging and differing significantly from the ways in which it is used and understood in other contexts. Morse and Clark (CD:7) discuss GTM sampling, distinguishing between sampling in qualitative and quantitative inquiry, then further distinguishing GTM sampling from other qualitative forms.

> We argue that sampling is not a procedure that is delegated for locating subjects who represent the population at the beginning of the study, as it is in quantitative inquiry. Rather, in qualitative inquiry, the goal of sampling is to represent the

phenomenon. In grounded theory, it is a procedural tool that is integral to the entire research process, with the goal of attaining excellent data that enables to development and verification of an abstract and generalizable theory.

The key to sampling derives from what they term 'the concept of adequacy'. For qualitative research this is based on the relevance of the sample to the phenomenon under investigation, in sharp contrast to sampling in a quantitative study. For GTM, however, they stress that sampling is part of the process of what they term 'emergent design', a key feature of GTM, implying that researchers cannot be expected to know from the outset the types of samples that will be required in later stages of research. In this regard, GTM sampling is a 'situated action' (see Bryant, 2017, Chapter 11; Suchman, 1984) as opposed to one that can be prepared and planned from the start. In Morse and Clark's terms 'sampling strategies must be flexible ... used for developing the concepts, as well as constructing and confirming the theory', the process as a whole being 'integrated into the process of inquiry'.

Morse and Clark stress that the issue of sampling extends into the latter stages of GTM research, so that it encompasses use of literature and 'sampling from the library, including research on the topic conducted by others', developing 'generalizability to other concepts, by linking to other theories, experiences and populations'. They offer a range of heuristic devices, including how to 'sample for process', and how to establish one's concepts beyond the specific research context itself. They also address the issue of the role of researchers, taking into account aspects such as ethnicity and culture.

Terminology

Although some of the acronyms used for variants of GTM may cause confusion, this is remedied once the full expression of the acronym is confirmed, even if it is unique or specific to that text. GTM terminology, however, is another matter. Charmaz included a glossary in *Constructing Grounded Theory* (Charmaz, 2006, 2014a), and in the 2007 volume we incorporated these definitions in our expanded *Discursive Glossary* (Bryant & Charmaz, 2007a). We have revised this glossary for *Current Developments* (Bryant & Charmaz, 2019), but readers should be aware that writers adhere to their own terms and we did not seek to impose any form of standardized terminology. To paraphrase Crossman and Noma (CD:29), students have to navigate the tricky spaces of GTM texts.

In her comments on an earlier version of Friese's chapter, Charmaz noted that differing uses of terms such as codes and coding are an ongoing issue for GTM, now made more complex with the advent of CAQDAS. Friese also argues:

> Some 'codes', however, may never be methodological; they simply serve organizational purposes to support data retrieval. Further, the code system needs to be structured in a way to be able to use more advanced software tools later in the analysis. This is based on technical requirements of the software and might lead to the impression to remodel GT to QDA. The latter would only be the case if the analyst was only tagging the data without writing, and thus not translating the underlying methodology in the intended way.

There is also the vexed question of the relationship between the terms code, category, and concept. In 2007 we discussed the different ways in which these terms were used in the GTM literature. In some cases, one text uses 'code' where another opts for 'category'; similarly, for 'category' and 'concept'. This applied not only to texts by different authors, but also to different texts by the same author(s). The early GTM texts referred to a 'core category' as the outcome of a GTM study, but also referred to a grounded theory as a study of a concept; Glaser himself argues (CD:21) that GTM 'is itself a grounded theory with conceptualization being the core category': GTM is 'about developing conceptualizations'.

I continue to opt for a hierarchy moving from codes at the most basic and numerous level, through to a smaller number of categories, arriving at a single core concept, or perhaps two or three core concepts (Bryant, 2017, Chapter 5). Others, including Charmaz, employ the original sequence of code → concept → category. Regardless of the specific approach being employed, researchers will end up with numerous codes which need to be organized so that some sense can be made from the data. Friese makes this point with respect to CAQDAS 'codes', but it also applies to manual coding. Many GTM researchers report that their initial studies, when they are open coding, can result in an unmanageable number of codes, often in the hundreds. Although potentially bewildering, researchers usually find that they can group these, and provide a coherent and persuasive account for so doing. Charmaz (2014a) recommends assessing how analytic codes subsume more descriptive codes and coding to develop analytic codes that can be raised to tentative categories.

Different researchers may well develop different categories from the same data, but that is a 'feature' rather than a 'bug' – i.e. the process has to be understood interpretatively, involving a dialogue between researchers and data. Different researchers will have distinctive dialogues with the data, steering their investigations accordingly. Multiple researchers will complicate but also enrich these ongoing dialogues. Researchers may also develop different categories and concepts from the same data, as Glaser and Strauss did for *Awareness* (1965b), then subsequently for *Time* (1968).

The outcome of a successful grounded theory study is a concept or some limited number of related concepts – in either case the term 'conceptualization' seems the most appropriate. Glaser (2004) uses the term as a distinguishing feature of GTM, which is 'straightforward conceptualization integrated into theory – a set of plausible, grounded hypotheses'. Corbin and Strauss (2008, p. 263) likewise: 'the point in analysis when all categories are well developed in terms of properties, dimensions, and variations. Further data gathering and analysis add little new to the *conceptualization*, though variations can always be discovered' (emphasis added).

The gerund form *conceptualizing* is not defined in many GTM texts, including the 2007 volume, but is included in *Current Developments* (Bryant & Charmaz, 2007a, 2019). Strauss and Corbin clearly noticed its relevance, arguing that it was the 'first step in theory building' (1998, p. 103) – a form of abstracting. This implies that it comes into force in the middle and later stages of GTM-oriented research, after preliminary or open coding of initial data.

Charmaz offers the following characterization of 'categorizing' that seems to encompass 'conceptualizing' in all but name.

Categorizing: the analytic step in grounded theory of selecting certain codes as having overriding significance or abstracting common themes and patterns in several codes into an analytic concept. As the researcher categorizes, he or she raises the conceptual level of the analysis from description to a more abstract, theoretical level. The researcher then tries to define the properties of the category, the conditions under which it is operative, the conditions under which it changes, and its relation to other categories. Grounded theorists make their most significant theoretical categories into the concepts of their theory. (Charmaz, 2006, 2014a, p. 341)

Charmaz continues to use the initial GTM hierarchy, with codes leading to categories, and finally one or more core concepts. Her terms follow the traditions of her discipline, in which relationships between concepts are used in theorizing.

Our introduction to the 2007 volume referred to several different uses of these terms, and there is no obvious resolution to this. Instead, I caution readers to satisfy themselves that they understand how the terms are used and how they relate to one another, in any specific text. Also, that they themselves, when writing about their research, clarify their use of the terms, striving for consistency and coherence.

Coding and CAQDAS: Text mining

Mitsuyuki Inaba and Hisako Kakai (CD:16) refer to 'coding' in the context both of GTM and what they term GTxA: 'an innovative approach to qualitative data analysis called the grounded text mining approach'. They argue that there are three key advantages to this approach, linking GTM directly to CAQDAS. The first is that it helps balance 'viewpoints in theory construction', i.e. 'the two perspectives of depth and breadth in understanding text data by combining the GTM, which is based on the constructivist paradigm, and the visualization of text resources via text mining'. Second, this enhances 'transparency in the data analysis process', allowing others to recognize the steps taken in moving from the initial data to the higher-level abstractions. Finally, building on these two features, the overall 'cognitive load of the researcher' can be reduced.

They offer various caveats relating to the use of CAQDAS and Big Data, echoing Bryant and Raja (2014), where we cautioned against reliance on algorithmic approaches to data – whether or not they involve computer technology. They admit that GTxA is time-consuming, in terms of the initial effort required to learn the CAQDAS package; also, that since 'GTxA uses the methods of both the GTM and text mining, more time is required to obtain the final result compared with conducting each analysis independently'. Andrea Gorra makes a similar point regarding time (CD:15).

Method, methodology, tool

Johnson and Walsh (CD:25) point out that '[S]ince GT was first described in 1967 through the epochal collaboration of Glaser and Strauss, GT has been understood by various authors as a technique, a method, a methodology, a framework, a paradigm, or as a meta-theory of inductive research design'. This is much to the consternation of students looking for clarification rather than confusion from the research methods literature. To resolve this, I have offered my own perspective on the relationship between terms such as method, methodology, model, tool, and technique – also strategy, approach, and design – with regards to research (Bryant, 2017, Chapter 2), but others will have their own, differing approaches.

Many discussions use the terms 'method' and 'methodology' inter-changeably, and unless otherwise specified they can be understood synonymously. Flick, who has written a number of important and authori-tative texts on qualitative research (e.g. Flick, 2008a, 2008b, 2014a, 2014b, 2015), opts for the term 'research design'. He argues that the term 'design' is a fluid concept and highly appropriate in the context of research since researchers need to be ready to change their strategy and approach as their investigations develop. I have argued similarly that research*ing* needs to be understood as a series of 'situated actions' (Bryant, 2017, Chapter 11). Flick (CD:6) quotes Charles Ragin:

> Research design is a plan for collecting and analyzing evidence that will make it possible for the investigator to answer whatever questions he or she has posed. The design of an investigation touches almost all aspects of the research, from the minute details of data collection to the selection of the techniques of data analysis. (Ragin, 1994, p. 191)

Strübing uses the term 'research style', arguing that the

> strong ties between Strauss's pragmatist predisposition and his methodological perspective show up in the operational mode of Grounded Theory as a *research style*: The iterative-cyclical process mode he proposes (Strauss & Corbin, 1994) mirrors Dewey's model of problem-solving – as does his notion of theory as a 'never-ending process' (Glaser & Strauss, 1967: 40). Also, the idea of theoretical sensitivity resonates with Mead's concept of perspective (Mead, 1932/1959). (emphasis added)

Flick also quotes from *Boys in White* (1961), where Becker et al. claim that:

> In one sense, our study had no design. That is, we had no well-worked-out set of hypotheses to be tested, no data-gathering instruments, purposely designed to secure information relevant to these hypotheses, no set of analytic proce-dures specified in advance. Insofar as the term 'design' implies these features of elaborate prior planning, our study had none. If we take the idea of design in a larger and looser sense, using it to identify those elements of order, system, and consistency our procedures did exhibit, our study had a design. We can say

what this was by describing our original view of our problem, our theoretical and methodological commitments, and the way these affected our research and were affected by it as we proceeded. (1961, p. 17)

This statement hints at some characteristics of GTM, describing the balance between being open to surprise and the unexpected in the early stages of research, but also conducting the study in a disciplined and rigorous manner, combining theoretical and methodological sensitivities. The statement also indicates the strong continuity between Chicago School ethnography and grounded theory.

Sharlene Hesse-Biber and Hillary Flowers (CD:24) focus on the added-value that feminist grounded theoretical approaches can bring to mixed methods research designs, aiming for combinations that are 'integrative' and 'reciprocal'. Through case studies, they establish how using GTM can support feminist research goals, observing that feminist principles can stretch and expand GTM-in-use, leading to more profound research. Moreover, building on the reciprocal effects between feminist principles and GTM strengthens each and makes the results more powerful, credible, resonant, and useful (Charmaz's terms).

In contrast, Johnson and Walsh (CD:25) seek to locate GTM against current discussion of mixed methods, making a distinction between mixed methods research (MMR) and multimethods research (MR). They provide an overview of current concerns, and demonstrate

how careful and thoughtful combining of grounded theory and mixed methods research can result in an exciting methodology that we call mixed grounded theory (MGT). MGT is an approach to research that relies on ideas found in grounded theory and mixed methods research.

Early statements by Strauss and his colleagues, such as that given earlier, indicate that the idea of mixing methods – i.e. combining aspects of one method with another – has always been a key aspect of good research practice. Consequently, building on Glaser and Strauss's work, I have coined the term *methodological sensitivity*, in recognition that virtually all research involves plans and intentions with regards to the application of a combination of methods, tools, and techniques. There are few, if any, examples of unalloyed application of any single method, since methods, research plans, designs, and strategies usually falter at the first contact with the research setting.

Johnson and Walsh would argue that in many cases this is an example of multimethod rather than mixed methods research. Their discussion demonstrates the need for researchers to understand the importance of articulating their overall approach, including the forms of data that are encompassed, and the forms of analysis that are employed.

Discovery included the subtitle *Strategies for Qualitative Research*, but this never precluded use of quantitative *data*. On the other hand, Glaser and Strauss rarely, if ever, refer to such data. Glaser's dictum 'All is data' indicates that all forms of data are amenable to GTM, and in 2008, in *Doing Quantitative Grounded Theory*, he argued that the GTM researchers should not shy away from 'the rich meanings to be found and grounded in secondary quantitative measurement' (Glaser, 2008, p. 89). Grounded theories can be generated from incorporation of quantitative data, including that collected by others in previous research exercises. In referring to this as '*quantitative GT*', however, Glaser introduces potential confusion, since it may be thought that this is a distinct form of GTM, rather than strengthening and clarifying the case that GTM researchers can and should consider using all forms of data, and in virtually any combination.

Johnson and Walsh refer to the issue of triangulation, defining it as 'the convergence of findings across methods', something that occurs both in mixed method and multimethod research. Flick, likewise, discusses triangulation, tracing the concept in some senses from Glaser and Strauss's term 'slices of data'.[3]

> If we take again the first edition of this *Handbook* (Bryant & Charmaz, 2007) as a reference, it looks like triangulation is also a concept which is not too prominent in grounded theory discussions about methodology. However, the ideas behind triangulation are not too far away from what is done in grounded theory research. *The main idea of triangulation is to extend the research by using several methods, differing theories or multiple researchers.* The resulting extension of data and interpretations in the process is seen as a contribution to make research and results more credible and fruitful. (Flick, CD:6, emphasis added)

In so doing, Flick introduces the issue of how multiple researchers interact in a research project. In this regard, 'slices of data' involves understanding that different researchers may well *slice* the same data in different ways, perhaps as a result of their individual backgrounds, training, or agendas. Again, this is something that underlines the importance of people's theoretical and methodological sensitivities.

As has already been noted, Glaser and Strauss hardly addressed the ways in which they collaborated in their work on death and dying. Collaboration is a topic barely broached in research methods texts. Flick (CD:6) quotes Hammersley and Atkinson (1995, p. 24) 'who argue in the context of ethnography that "research design should be a reflexive process which operates throughout every stage of a project"'. Katja Mruck and Günter Mey devote their entire chapter (CD:23) to a discussion on reflexivity, delineating, and clarifying its place in the research process, and explaining how it affects outcomes. They offer researchers a list of concerns that individual and multiple researchers should consider during their projects. But empirical discussions of how reflexivity leads multiple researchers to interact, discuss, and compromise during the research process have not really figured to any significant degree in the research methods literature.

Duckles et al. (CD:31) offer some important insights on this topic, including their statement of how they work together, seeking to incorporate other research participants.

> We code both individually and as a team, develop consensus categories, review our data to saturate the categories and build themes. We reach into academic research literature, but also into local literature, stories and knowledge as part of our constant comparative methods and processes of abduction, as we challenge, revise, and enrich our analysis.

They include guidance showing how collaboration between academic and community-based researchers can:

1. build on local knowledge and address both local issues and systemic change through iterative cycles of research;
2. acknowledge and integrate the emergent tensions in community-based participatory action research to generate both practical solutions;
3. start from the principles of people in the community (Afrocentric philosophies were crucial in their work);
4. use symbolic interactionism as a guiding perspective, and abductive analysis as a methodological strategy. (my paraphrase)

Crossman and Noma (CD:29) discuss how multiple researchers collaborate using GTM, and several other contributors to *Current Developments* (Bryant & Charmaz, 2019) refer to the need to acknowledge researchers' differing cultural and linguistic backgrounds. As will be seen below, however, terms such as 'culture', 'paradigm', and 'indigeneity' need to be treated with care and critical insight. If pushed too far they lead to the paradox that irked readers of Thomas Kuhn's work, and infamously Kuhn himself, namely the problem of 'the incommensurability of paradigms'.[4] Aspects of this can often come to the fore in the interactions between students and their supervisors, a topic discussed below in addressing student and learning issues.

Methodologizing: GTM and methodological positioning

Given all these developments, variants, and other off-shoots, it is not surprising that Reichertz (CD:13) argues that there is 'no central reference text' for GTM, nor 'a binding canonization'. He sees this as 'both a blessing and a curse', arising from the method being freed from 'a specific form of working'. The 'blessing' is that GTM researchers are now guided by 'general principles – which makes adaptation to the respective subject matter considerably easier'. The converse of this, however, is it facilitates something of a free-for-all, allowing anyone 'to perform a somehow "open" and "data-oriented" analysis [and] to flag their respective practice as "grounded theory"'.

As Strauss and Corbin feared in the 1990s, GTM is now 'in vogue', but whereas they worried about it then becoming 'old-hat', it has, on the contrary, become a *fashion label*, claimed and invoked extravagantly and all-too-often speciously. (Crossman and Noma (CD:29) use the phrase 'methodological consumerism', albeit in a slightly different context.) Glaser reacts to such tenuous claims, using various epithets for what he sees as invalid or counterfeit forms of GTM. Unfortunately, he casts his net indiscriminately, often aiming reproaches at variants of GTM from which he wishes to distance his own, but which are perfectly valid and robust forms of the method itself. The origins of this can be found in the earliest works of Glaser and Strauss, where they needed to clear the ground for GTM, and hence distinguish it from other positions with which it might be confused. Glaser and Strauss, Strauss and Corbin, and Glaser on his own have coined numerous terms from which GTM needed to be distanced, including 'mindless empiricism', 'mere description', 'full conceptual description', failure to achieve 'conceptual density', and 'grounded description'. Glaser has also described what others would consider valid variants of GTM as 'remodelling' the method or examples of 'jargonizing' – applying this term to 25 of the 27 chapters of the 2007 volume (Glaser, 2009).

The result is that GTM researchers need to position their use of the method against this rich, flexible, but bewildering and potentially misleading array of possibilities. In my grounded theory study of a large number of recent GTM papers, I developed the core concept of 'methodologizing', and a sub-concept of 'methodological positioning'. Methodologizing refers to

> the ways in which researchers link their actual approach to other methods ... [the] process of *methodologizing* includes discussion of the scope of GTM, reference to philosophical issues such as induction, deduction, and concern with ontological and epistemological topics – a common indication of this will be in reference to 'research paradigms'. ... [also the sub-concept of 'positioning', including the statements researchers offer] relating to aspects or features of GTM – also to omissions or references to canonical or authoritative texts and issues. (see Bryant, 2017, Chapter 14, Box 14.2, p. 295)

Reichertz's point regarding the lack of a central text for GTM is understandable, if contentious. In the 1990s it was common to read research papers and doctoral theses that referred only to the second edition of Strauss and Corbin (1998). This is less common now, but I have found in various workshops, seminars, and doctoral examinations that although there is almost universal reference made to *Discovery*, the book itself has been read, at best, in a cursory manner. Ludwik Fleck argued that the existence of a central text is critical in establishing substantive and methodological aspects of a subject area

> ...a judgment about the existence or non-existence of a phenomenon belongs, in a democratic collective, to a numerous council, not to an individual. The textbook changes the subjective judgment of an author into a proven fact. It will be united with the entire system of science, it will henceforward be recognized and taught, it will become a foundation of further facts and the guiding principle of what will be seen and applied (1936, VI). (SEP entry on Fleck, *Stanford Encyclopedia of Philosophy*, n.d.)

Fleck refers to a single text, but with regard to GTM it would be more appropriate to consider which set of texts are 'recognized and taught'; different selections indicating which variant of GTM is under consideration and use. *Discovery* itself is clearly 'recognized' in this sense, its inclusion being commonplace in most discussions of GTM or GTM-oriented research. *Awareness* and *Time* are cited as widely. My grounded theory of GTM papers (Bryant, 2017, Chapter 14) found that the inclusion and omission of

certain GTM texts was a reasonably accurate indicator of the methodological position taken by the researchers involved; this supports Fleck's
argument when applied to a set of texts rather than a specific one.

Since 2007 the volume of GTM literature has burgeoned. In many
respects this is to be welcomed as researchers can now consult numerous
sources if they want to learn and develop their ideas about GTM. Several
introductory texts, and also chapters on GTM in handbooks and collections, are devoted to research methods in general or qualitative methods in
particular. Also, a large and growing number of research papers and completed doctoral theses are available online. These provide something of a
mixed blessing. On the plus side, they provide researchers with archetypes
for GTM-oriented research that can assist those seeking guidance with
regards to both the process and the presentation for their research –
with the caveat that the actual process is accurately and candidly described
in the publication. There is, however, the danger that such exemplars
will become seen as standard models to be mimicked with little or no
reflection on applicability and relevance. This issue arises with all forms
of research and is not confined to GTM or qualitative research. Indeed,
looking across the range of GTM outputs – journal papers, theses, and the
like – there seems to be a varied and stimulating range of formats and structures. Some PhD theses are presented as straightforward reports, others
are interspersed with detailed memos, extracts from the data, and various
types of visualizations. Some PhD students strive to offer novel formats for
their work, including the use of 'story-line' and narrative accounts, and even
extended dialogues. Some of the ways in which GTM research has and might
be presented are referred to in Chapter 6 on Student and Learning Issues.

A family divergence

The extended metaphor of family resemblances and genealogy encom-
passes the 'family divergence' that developed in the 1990s. Publication
of Strauss and Corbin's *Basics of Qualitative Research* drew a vehement
response from Glaser, prompting publication of *Basics of Grounded Theory*
(Glaser, 1992), where he distanced himself from the views expressed by
Strauss and Corbin, claiming their book represented a move away from
GTM while masquerading as an articulation of the method. He castigated
Strauss for the 'immoral undermining' (p. 121) of GTM, arguing that Strauss
was never really in tune with GTM proper, having remained wedded to

what Glaser termed the method of 'full conceptual description'. Some have referred to this as a dispute between Glaser and Strauss, but Strauss, who died in 1996, never responded to Glaser. The chapter on grounded theory published in the first edition of Denzin and Lincoln's *Handbook of Qualitative Research* includes a footnote that might be understood to refer obliquely to Glaser's account (Strauss & Corbin, 1994):

> AUTHORS' NOTE: This summary statement represents the authors' views as participants in, contributors to, and observers of grounded theory's evolution. *Others who have been part of this intellectual movement will differ in their views of some points made here and the relative importance we give them.* (Strauss & Corbin, 1994, p. 273, emphasis added)

Many of the chapters, both in the 2007 *Handbook* and *Current Developments* (Bryant & Charmaz, 2007a, 2019), present explanations of these events that are couched in ameliorative rather than combative terms. One view is that both Glaser, and Strauss – initially on his own, then later together with Corbin – were, in their different ways seeking to support students with theoretical coding, and more generally moving from commonplace description to theoretical insights and conceptualization. Strauss and Corbin, writing in 1994, argued that although many researchers were 'claiming use of GTM', they were often 'failing to accomplish more than a fairly mundane level of coding, certainly not moving on to theoretical coding, and subsequently to generating theoretical statements'. Glaser has consistently made similar statements. Glaser's response was couched in terms of his 'coding families', which first appeared in *Theoretical Sensitivity* (1978). Strauss and Corbin proposed their 'coding paradigm' in the 1990s, as a remedy to the repeated failure of researchers to move from the fracturing that results in 'substantive' coding to the articulation of more integrative conceptualizations.

Glaser criticized Strauss and Corbin for 'forcing' the outcome with their coding paradigm, but others have pointed out that Glaser's coding families are incoherent, bewildering, and can also encourage forcing the data into a particular coding family. Thus Kelle (CD:3) argues that 'researchers with a broad theoretical background knowledge and a longstanding experience in the application of theoretical terms will certainly not need such a list'. On the other hand, he goes on to state that the coding paradigm 'may be much more helpful for researchers with limited experience in conceptualizing empirical data in theoretical terms', largely because it is more explicit. But this is also the reason why Glaser's criticisms hit home. Kelle concludes that ultimately 'Glaser's critique that the coding paradigm may lead to the forcing of categories on the data cannot be dismissed'. Kelle characterizes the issue as emanating from the 'antagonism between *emergence* and *theoretical sensitivity*'.

Although I do not have extensive evidence regarding how doctoral and other early-career researchers develop their concepts, I do have substantial familiarity in teaching, supervising, and examining numerous students – currently 50+ GTM-type PhDs. Based on this small but select sample, it appears that the intricacies of moving from low-level, embedded codes to higher-level, more abstract ones that are then related to one another as part of a conceptual model or theory, does not present a significant problem. Moreover, few if any have used Strauss and Corbin's coding paradigm or Glaser's coding families; those who have tried mostly report disappointment in their respective practicalities.

On the other hand, Charmaz has found grounded theory studies, across many different fields, that fail to offer conceptual analyses, much less a cogent theory, sometimes trying to disguise this by presenting their weak conceptualizations as neologisms in the form of gerunds, but which in fact are nothing more than everyday terms to which the suffix '-izing' has been added.[5] I suspect that many such cases of inadequate research are largely the result of poor GTM research practice and/or lack of mentoring or understanding, in which case guidance on theoretical coding would not really provide any effective remedy. A well-grounded study on GTM-in-use would be enormously helpful in shedding more light on this.

It may be that what was a common problem in the 1980s and 1990s has now largely been resolved or simply dissipated. Students do often find themselves 'flooded with data', but in most cases they manage to progress to develop higher-level abstractions that form the basis of theoretical accounts. Moreover, those who encounter problems with this transition often continue to do so even if they try to adopt the strategies proposed by Glaser or Strauss and Corbin. Neither the coding paradigm nor coding families quite seem to fit the bill.

Both Strauss and Corbin and Glaser combined the justification for their 'remedies' with criticism of researchers claiming largely or wholly unwarranted use of GTM. For this group, neither the coding paradigm nor the coding families will resolve anything. As Strauss and Corbin observed in

1994, 'a child once launched is very much subject to a combination of its origins and the evolving contingencies of life. Can it be otherwise with a methodology?' The problem of disobedient or misbehaving children persists!

Another explanation for the Glaser–Strauss divergence centres on abduction. Thanks to Kathy's anecdote (Charmaz, 2014a, p. 202), we know that Strauss already saw GTM as an abductive method in the 1960s, whereas Glaser continues to stress only the inductive nature of GTM. Jane Gilgun (CD:5) discusses the deductive aspects of GTM, which may appear somewhat strange given the explicit rejection of orthodox social science research – characterized as hypothetico-deductive – in the early GTM texts, particularly *Discovery*. Gilgun, however, locates GTM against the background of Chicago School sociology, but in contrast to two other forms of analysis associated with Chicago. Her chapter focuses on:

> Deductive qualitative analysis (DQA), one of three approaches to research associated with the Chicago School of Sociology. The other two are GT and field research, which is descriptive in nature, and sometimes referred to as ethnographic research.

Gilgun explains that 'DQA is an updating of analytic induction ... an approach older than GT'. Unlike GTM, DQA and its predecessor – analytic induction – 'allows for qualitative hypothesis testing and theory testing as well as concept-guided descriptive research'. In both cases, such research begins with sensitizing concepts, which, Gilgun notes, was 'traditional in the Chicago School for decades before Blumer (1969) gave them a name (Gilgun, 1999, 2005, 2016)'. All three forms of research 'produce findings that are grounded in data on which findings are based'.

Reichertz (CD:13) argues that GTM 'was to a very small extent abductive from the start and has become more and more abductive in its more recent stages. The controversy within GT can be characterized, at least in part, as one between induction and abduction'. The role of abduction in GTM is now far more widely understood than was the case even at the time of the 2007 *Handbook*. Strauss certainly understood this, even if he did not share the full ramifications with his colleagues or discuss it in his writings on GTM.

A later chapter addresses 'Student and Learning Issues' specifically, but I have already remarked on the ways in which the various disputes, divergences, and differences can be perplexing for those seeking to understand, gain familiarity with, and use GTM. GTM now comes in several variants, and even the founding texts are losing their canonical status. Graduate students and others should be able to contend with this. They need to read widely and make sense of how the method might be incorporated into their own research activities: developing and demonstrating *methodological sensitivity*. Those writing about GTM, however, need to understand that they can hinder this, particularly if they merely offer chastisement and censure, failing to offer clear and respectful accounts of positions with which they may well disagree, but which still warrant attention (see the earlier discussion of Rapoport's rules).

Summary of 'core characteristics' of GTM

The Senior Editor's Introduction to *Current Developments* (Bryant, 2019) includes my summary of what I consider the 'essences' of GTM; it is reproduced here to conclude this section. (Most of the key terms are included in the *Discursive Glossary* (2019) in *Current Developments*.)

- **Coding-cum-analysis-cum-memoing** – the form and strategy for coding in GTM was and remains innovative in many ways, including its starting point, and its iterative nature;
- Also the link to **memoing**, which, although largely absent from the earliest writings, is now a key feature;
- **Substantive and formal theory generation** – this developed in part from Merton's idea that research should aim to provide theories of the middle range. In contrast to mid-20th century preoccupations with hypothetical structural explanations of whole societies, Merton (1957) advocated constructing theories to explain empirical problems – both Substantive Grounded Theories and Formal Grounded Theories are examples of this;[6]
- **Purposive/convenience sampling followed by theoretical sampling** – qualitative sampling was and still is misunderstood, particularly by those whose research experience and expertise is derived largely or wholly from a quantitative background; GTM offers a basis for clarifying sampling issues for qualitative research in general;
- **Theoretical saturation** – often seen as a weakness of GTM, but, used correctly, it is in fact a strength of the method, since, unlike many methods, it offers the rationale for claiming to have reached an interim end-point for a research endeavour;

- **Use of the literature** – initially to establish the basis for the research but, far more importantly, to refer to and engage with the relevant literature as an additional and critical form of data against which interim or later analyses can be positioned – this is what is referred to as theoretical coding;
- **Criteria – fit, grab, work, modifiability**; and also Charmaz's **credibility, originality, resonance, usefulness**;
- **Openness to serendipity**;
- **Pragmatism** – particularly the ways in which GTM now has to be understood as a method for what I have termed '***enacting abstraction and abduction***'.

Some of these are important for many other, if not all other, methods, but several are specific to GTM, and their combination is unique to GTM. More critically, taken together, they embody a distinctively persuasive, coherent, rigorous, and effective method for undertaking qualitative research.

I do not expect all writers on GTM, nor all readers of this monograph and of *Current Developments* to concur with this account; indeed, I would be amazed if that was the case. Glaser and Strauss, particularly in *Discovery*, were keen to challenge their peers, and stir up controversy and debate. Those of us wishing to follow in their footsteps need to do likewise, but we must take care to understand the important distinction made by Albert Camus (2000 [1951]) between the *historical rebel* and *metaphysical rebel*. The former aims at perfection, and some set of 'absolute values'; the latter accepts the absurdity of the drama of social existence and the 'unreasonable silence of the world', recognizing social existence and any attempts to encapsulate it as uncertain, complex, and chaotic. GTM is the research method for metaphysical rebels *par excellence*, so it is no wonder that it remains beset by controversy and discord, both from within and without; yet it continues to provide an inimitable spur and support for challenging and innovative research and conceptualization.

GTM in the age of Big Data

CAQDAS – Computer Aided/Assisted Qualitative Data Analysis

The 2007 volume did not have a chapter devoted to computer-aided analysis, or anything on the ways in which digital technologies are and might be used in GTM (Bryant & Charmaz, 2007a). One was planned, but unfortunately the chapter was not submitted. In 2007 this may not have been a major omission, but now it certainly would be. CAQDAS is now an inescapable aspect of qualitative research; indeed, Friese (CD:14) wonders how anyone can contemplate data analysis *without* using it in some form or other. This position is reinforced by Gorra (CD:15), who refers to claims that the millennial generation, having, in Dan Tapscott's (2008) terms, 'grown up digital', will undertake research assuming that computer-based technology is always at-hand, ready to be incorporated into the research process in any number of ways.

Glaser has consistently argued that GT researchers should not use computer-based facilities for coding and analysis, correctly pointing out that researchers cannot and should not rely on technology as a substitute for their own insights and skills, developed from experience in GT data analysis. But as both Friese and Gorra demonstrate, things have developed rapidly in this regard, and the manner in which CAQDAS and related technologies can and have been incorporated in highly successful GT research cannot be ignored; on the contrary, there are lessons here for everyone to heed even if they have no intention of using CAQDAS.

There is a certain irony in the term CAQDAS itself in the context of GTM. The term that it encompasses, QDA (Qualitative Data Analysis), was used by Strauss and Glaser, both in their joint work and their later, distinct publications, as a form of deprecation. From their earliest writings, Glaser and Strauss were at pains to stress that many forms of qualitative research did not, and could not, lead to theory generation. For example, in *Discovery* they argue that '[D]escription, ethnography, fact-finding, verification (call them what you will) ... cannot generate sociological theory' (1967, p. 7). Strauss often referred disdainfully to 'mere description'. Glaser (CD:21) has used various terms in a similar manner, including QDA and Grounded Description. In the meantime, however, QDA has taken on a life of its own, so it is now seen as a neutral and generic term covering all forms of qualitative analysis and hence as the basis for CAQDAS. Friese (CD:14) herself distinguishes between CAQDAS and QDA, preferring the former since it incorporates the idea that the software 'assists' the analysis/analyst; the prime activity is undertaken by the researcher(s) and not the software.

QDA software implies that the software is doing the analysis instead of being a tool aiding the researcher (who still must do the thinking). Automation is certainly an issue these days given the massive amounts of data available. But big data analysis is different from qualitative data analysis even if big data may consist of qualitative, i.e., non-numeric data (Friese, 2016). Thus, we need to distinguish between the analysis of qualitative data and qualitative data analysis, whereby GT is a form of the latter.

Friese demonstrates extensive familiarity, skill, and insight with the software, including NVivo,[7] MAXQDA, and Atlas.ti,[8] offering detailed descriptions of differing implementations of a case study drawn from the work of Strauss in the 1980s and Corbin more recently.

Charmaz commented on an early version of Friese's chapter as follows:

> Your chapter captured my interest and raised all kinds of foundational questions about GT. Readers will not only find it to be helpful in understanding the software but also in asking fundamental questions about the grounded theory method.

> You do an excellent job in showing how researchers can use the programs to handle myriad details. The capability of the programs for synthesizing data is unassailable. The extent to which they help in scaling up to theory is less apparent to me. What struck me is that what stands as a theoretical category or concept differs markedly between grounded theorists. That may be an artifact of using Strauss and Corbin's approach, which Glaser (1992) dismissed as 'full conceptual description'. Fundamental questions arise. What is a code? When and how do CAQDAS programs help the researcher to raise codes? How is theorizing distinguished from describing? What makes an analysis theoretical?

I have argued elsewhere (Bryant, 2014), and in a range of different contexts, that the introduction of digital technology often exposes the complexities of what have previously been seen as mundane or unexceptional activities and practices, and this is certainly the case with Friese's analysis of CAQDAS, as Charmaz's comments indicate.

Based on her work using CAQDAS over 20 years, Friese wonders how anyone can avoid the technology: 'I can hardly imagine how one would handle the expected data material manually, and how to keep track of it'. On the other hand, she also points out that researchers with little or no experience of CAQDAS should not attempt to develop these skills as part of a research project: 'it is not a promising idea to begin learning to use a software tool because you have some data and now want to analyze them'.

This firmly resonates with Gorra's complementary chapter (CD:15). Gorra used NVivo, with mixed results, in her own PhD (see Bryant, 2017, Chapter 19), and was keen to find out how current PhD students are faring. Her approach was to do a grounded theory study of a small number of students, eventually producing the core concept of 'Movement: Keep Moving (Self, Mind, Data)'. One key aspect of her study is that all the students demonstrated *methodological sensitivity* as they experimented with different ways of 'interacting with the data', including consideration of possible tools such as CAQDAS. Gorra also found that '[B]ased on the analysis of my interviews with GT researchers, I believe that the many changes in the wider research environment, as discussed in the introduction, have had an impact on the actual practice of grounded theorizing'.

Gorra's core concept develops some of the ideas touched on by Friese. It encompasses three different aspects centred on 'time' in the context of doctoral research, including: the *length of time available* for the study; deciding whether or not to *invest time* to learn using a CAQDAS software package to gain potential time savings later on; and the time required for the actual *data analysis*.

In general, CAQDAS and a whole host of other technological developments must be recognized as having an extensive impact on the research process as a whole. Different researchers will find their own ways of incorporating available tools; in some cases, their strategies will prove to be dead-ends, but in others they will enhance the process and the outcomes. Peirce referred to *musement* in the research process; we now have *digital musement* as an important stage either early in the research process, as researchers experiment with their data and analytic codes, or later as they develop their concepts. Indeed, researchers should be encouraged to 'play' with the technology.

Data and Big Data

In the quote above, Friese distinguished between Big Data analysis and GTM analysis. Big Data is certainly a 'hot topic', and as such commonly over-sold. It has clear ramifications for GTM since it appears to be a way in which conclusions can *emerge* algorithmically through computerized processing of massive data sources. Some have argued that we no longer need theories, since we now have 'all the data', although few go as far as this (see Bryant, 2017, Chapter 16, for further discussion). Clearly, the opportunities offered by massive data sources need to be grasped, although the challenge they afford is far more directly a concern of quantitative research than qualitative. For instance, issues of sampling and the appropriate form of statistical analysis may simply not apply if the 'sample' is more-or-less the entire population, and the process of accounting for 'missing values' is a very different form of activity and analysis.

Some of the more outrageous claims regarding Big Data have been dismantled in our article in *First Monday* (Bryant & Raja, 2014; see also Bryant, 2017, Chapter 16), where we argue that far from Big Data eclipsing GTM and qualitative research and analysis, GTM actually provides a very clear and important corrective to some of the more outlandish claims of the Big Data proponents.

It might appear that claims along the lines of 'now we have all the data, there is no need for theories' is the logical conclusion of the idea that theories emerge from the data. I have always commended Glaser's slogan that 'all is data', in the sense that GTM researchers should potentially approach anything and everything as worthy bases for investigation – e.g. interviews, documents, observations, literature, websites, and so on. On the other hand, I have also cautioned against the idea that 'data is all', in the sense that concepts, models, and theories will somehow 'emerge' from the data itself – whatever its source or nature. The more extreme, enthusiastic, or provocative adherents of Big Data take this misunderstanding even further, echoing a Beatles lyric, so it is now understood as 'Big Data is all you need'. Clearly this is nonsense.

What Big Data claims fail to acknowledge is the role of human insight and conceptualization; exactly what the term *theoretical sensitivity* encompasses. Assertions that technology can do everything in this context are similar to those in the artifical intelligence (AI) community who claim that abduction can now be automated.

Inaba and Kakai (CD:16), describing their conception of GTxA (a grounded text mining approach), outline one way in which GTM researchers can use these technological advances:

> [GTxA is] an integrative, reflective, and cyclical process that obtains an overview of the text data (Step 1), completes a qualitative data analysis (Step 2), creates visualization and performs an analysis with text mining (Step 3), and then develops a meta-inference (Step 4). By cyclically repeating these steps, researchers obtain a deeper understanding of the text data.

But they stress that it is the researchers who develop and have to articulate this deeper understanding of the data; a process best explained in terms of a constructivist understanding of GTM. They concur with Bryant and Raja (2014), where we argue that both Big Data analysis (often termed Knowledge Discovery from Data) and GTM are 'instantiations of hermeneutics', envisaged not as a circle but rather as a 'spiral moving from an origin focused on the data towards ever higher levels of abstraction and conceptual reach'.[9]

Whatever GTM researchers might think and seek to do with regards to CAQDAS, Big Data, and other manifestations of digital technology, they need to pay them some cognizance. In the first instance considering how they might be of assistance, and also being prepared to respond to those who might challenge their findings from a perspective based on misuse and misunderstanding of 'Big Data' or other resources that fail to incorporate insight and theoretical sensitivity.

Images as data

Krzysztof Konecki (CD:17) takes the idea of 'all is data' one stage further, arguing that images can and should be amenable to GTM analysis. He develops Glaser and Strauss's metaphor of 'slices of data' with his concept of 'multi-slice imaginings', defined as a process that involves 'identifying the layers of image that should be analyzed (levels of creation, structure, presentation and reception of image)'. He argues that 'visual grounded theory' should be understood as a distinct way of doing GTM, and that this was already present to some extent in Clarke's situational analysis, which 'announced her departure from the basics of GT and instead proposed a concentration on situational analysis using visual materials' (Clarke, 2005).

One of Konecki's objectives is to draw attention to the processes involved in 'seeing' or 'observing'. He quotes Banks (2001, p. 7), 'Seeing is not natural, however much we might think it to be'. This aligns with the constructivist orientation which views interaction between 'researcher' and 'data' as an interpretative dialogue, applying to all forms of data, not only to images. GTM analysis necessarily involves interpretation and 'multi-slice imaginings', as discussed by Konecki.

Notes

1   Wertz et al. (2011) *Five Ways of Doing Qualitative Analysis* is a key source for those interested in learning more about different approaches.
2   See for instance, Saldana's book, which outlines several different forms of and approaches to coding (Saldana, 2015).
3   This term is common in the works of Glaser and Strauss, but its meaning is somewhat opaque. Kathy Charmaz was unsure of its precise meaning, but recalled Glaser and Strauss using it when discussing bits or fragments of data. I would

argue that the metaphor is, however, clearly distinct from this, since 'slicing' implies that the total data is somehow in one piece from which slices can be taken. I do not want to press this too far, but it does illustrate the ways in which the term 'data' was in many, important ways a key 'sensitizing concept' in the early GT writings, rather than a definitive one – see below.

4   Errol Morris relates an incident in his first year as one of Thomas Kuhn's graduate students. 'I asked him, "If paradigms are really incommensurable, how is history of science possible? Wouldn't we be merely interpreting the past in the light of the present? Wouldn't the past be inaccessible to us? Wouldn't it be *incommensurable?*" He started moaning. He put his head in his hands and was muttering, "He's trying to kill me. He's trying to kill me." And then I added, "... except for someone who imagines himself to be God." It was at this point that Kuhn threw the ashtray at me. And missed.' https://opinionator.blogs.nytimes.com/2011/03/06/the-ashtray-the-ultimatum-part-1/

5   For a discussion of GTM and gerunds, see A. Bryant (2017). Introduction to Part Three. In *Grounded Theory and Grounded Theorizing: Pragmatism in Research Practice*. Oxford: Oxford University Press.

6   Herbert Blumer (1954), a close colleague of Strauss in Chicago, similarly criticized 'grand theory' in his essay 'What is wrong with social theory?', *American Sociological Review*, 19, 3–10.

7   Confusion in conversation can arise in GTM since someone discussing NVivo codes may be understood to be referring to '*in vivo*' codes.

8   Atlas.ti is referred to in the UK as 'Atlas-tee-eye', but elsewhere, particularly in Germany where it was developed, as 'Atlas-tee'.

9   Hermeneutics is usually explained in terms of the hermeneutic circle – see https://plato.stanford.edu/entries/hermeneutics

3

GTM FROM A LOGICAL
POINT OF VIEW

Epistemology and ontology

It used to be the case that, in many disciplines, concerns about a research-er's epistemological stance were rarely more than nugatory. It was widely assumed that all researchers shared similar assumptions – essentially that scientific research was best accomplished by objective, disinterested, empir-ical work aimed at discovering 'the facts'. Not too far removed from Charles Dickens' caricature of English education in the Victorian era, embodied in Mr Gradgrind.

> NOW, what I want is, Facts. Teach these boys and girls nothing but Facts. Facts alone are wanted in life. Plant nothing else, and root out everything else. You can only form the minds of reasoning animals upon Facts: nothing else will ever be of any service to them. This is the principle on which I bring up my own chil-dren, and this is the principle on which I bring up these children. Stick to Facts, sir! (Dickens, *Hard Times*, 1854)[1]

Schatzman commended Glaser and Strauss for pushing researchers into making clear and articulate methodological commitments. The work of Thomas Kuhn (1962 & 1970) had an even greater impact, leading research-ers to consider and articulate their epistemological orientation. Yet many researchers, particularly those in what are termed 'the hard sciences', sim-ply carried on as before. Those employing qualitative methods, particularly in the social and human sciences, however, were expected to broach the issue at some point, and doctoral students in particular are now expected to address epistemological issues when discussing their method/methodology.

I take the view that, while commendable to some extent, it seems somewhat churlish to expect doctoral students to grapple with and clarify topics that remain highly contentious and unresolved even for erudite and experienced philosophers. As such, I advocate serious consideration of *epistemological avoidance*, albeit recognizing that this is not always a feasible option (see below).

In various discussions introducing and developing Constructivist GTM, Kathy Charmaz and I have sought to expose the ways in which pre-existing variants – including Glaser and Strauss's joint work, as well as their later distinct writings – were misleading in their epistemological claims; often with distinctly positivist assumptions and ramifications: Charmaz's chapter in the second edition of *The Handbook of Qualitative Research* being the *fons et origo* of this critique (Charmaz, 2000). Prior to this, the GTM position on such topics was largely one of *epistemological evasion* – the matter was not addressed at all.

Subsequent to Charmaz's and my writings, however, Glaser, and those who support his position, have responded by claiming that GTM is able to align with any and every epistemological orientation; a position I refer to as *epistemological indifference* (Glaser, 2002). Unfortunately, such cryptic catch-all claims evade the real complexities. If researchers are required or feel the need to declare and discuss their epistemological stance, then they must be able to offer some substantiation, perhaps in the form of an appeal to a set of authoritative statements, simultaneously observing that other sources argue an alternative or opposing opinion. Some writers on GTM – and other methods – seem highly concerned about the links between a researcher's stance on epistemology/ontology and the research strategy/process/methods that they then follow. This is more complex when more than one researcher is involved, particularly if researchers with differing – contrasting and even opposing – stances work in collaboration. Such collaborations might prove fruitful and insightful in the long run, if more time-consuming and troublesome in the short run.

Epistemological *indifference* is not a defensible position, neither is *evasion*. I do not advocate either, but I do understand and, in some contexts, recommend epistemological *avoidance*. Much as with paying tax, *avoidance* is legal and understandable; evasion is neither; indifference is hazardous. So too for doctoral researchers. It is perfectly reasonable to avoid detailed and complex discussions on 'the E and O words' (Bryant, 2017, Chapter 2).

In contrast, Charmaz does not support *avoidance*, but instead advocates a thorough engagement with epistemology since many disciplines and publications require clear statements on the topic. We concur, however, that researchers must be able to substantiate any epistemological claims they offer; with the caveat that such claims can often be implicit. For GTM this is particularly important since so many papers and other research outputs incorporate statements such as GTM is 'an inductive method', or 'we avoided all preconceptions', or 'the theory emerged from the data', all of which raise complex and important epistemological issues, without necessarily appearing to do so.

In my concluding discussion of 'the E and O words' I noted that:

> ... it is worth stressing that purity of method is no guarantee of value in research findings, or as Rorty (1977) has argued: 'Nothing is to be gained for an understanding of human knowledge by running together vocabularies in which we describe the causal antecedents of knowledge with those in which we offer justification of our claims to knowledge.' (Bryant, 2017, p. 56)

In other words, claimed adherence to a method is no substitute for effective insight.

GTM – an epistemological fairy-tale?

In his extended review of three books on the urban environment, Wacquant (2002) described GTM as 'an epistemological fairy-tale', a term often invoked in pejorative critiques of GTM. Wacquant applied this epithet both to GTM and 'diagnostic ethnography', a term 'coined by Duneier's Wisconsin colleague Erik Wright to characterize this inductivist, I-began-to-get-ideas-from-the-things-I-was-seeing-and-hearing-on-the-street approach to field-based inquiry'. Interestingly, he offers no references to GTM itself, seemingly assuming his sociological readership will understand the target of his gratuitous sideswipe.

Wacquant's review is symptomatic of the paradoxical relationship between GTM and sociology (see below). But for now, it is worth noting that Wacquant's sentiment regarding the inductivism of GTM seemed to be sufficiently commonplace in sociology in 2002 to require no further explanation. Such statements indicate a severe misinterpretation of GTM, perhaps an understandable failing at the time. Yet the full context of his comment reveals that he is actually praising Duneier for what can and should now be understood as a form of abduction largely emanating from GTM.

So he went about 'fishing' for questions to which these informants might have answers. But his problematic did not emerge inductively, as in the epistemological fairy tale of 'grounded theory' or 'diagnostic ethnography': it resulted from the projection, onto the sidewalk, of Duneier's personal interest in morality and 'respectability' (already evident in *Slim's Table*). Duneier must be given credit for the candor with which he acknowledges it: 'I hadn't formulated a precise research question. I had no theories that I wanted to test or reconstruct, and I didn't have a particular scholarly literature to which I knew I wanted to contribute. ... I sought mainly to diagnose the processes at work in this setting and to explain the observed patterns of interactions of people. I also have a general theme that guides me in collecting data *in all of my work: whether and how the people I am with are or are not struggling to live in accordance with standards of "moral" worth.*' (Wacquant, 2002, pp. 340–41, emphasis added)

Wacquant's short-hand dismissal of GTM occurs within the context of describing an approach that looks remarkably similar to a credible and well-crafted grounded theory study:

- no precise research question;
- specifically eschewing verification of existing theories;
- deliberately not scouring the literature;
- and seeking to explain general patterns based on a general view of what was going on in specific urban settings.

Indeed, Wacquant criticizes one of the books under review for artificially overlaying the 'narrative of deindustrialization and racial exclusion ... onto field descriptions ... [with a low] ratio of analysis to narrative and interview transcripts' – i.e. too much description and too little analysis; precisely the failings that Strauss and Corbin, and Glaser were already pointing out in 1990 when criticizing inadequate research masquerading as GTM. Wacquant's criticisms are aimed at the wrong target.

Epistemological metaphors – emergence, lens, extract, abstract

Although Strauss (Charmaz, 2014a; see also Strauss, 1987, p. 12) may have understood that GTM was 'abductive' – albeit that this key aspect was only more fully articulated, clarified, and made evident in recent times – the vocabulary used in the early GTM writings leads in other directions. Simplistic use of the term 'data', an *over-playing* (Strauss's term) of induction, and the ramifications of the precept that researchers should allow the theory to emerge from the data, are all imbued with a positivist epistemology and its ramifications. The metaphor of 'emerging' continues to plague discussion of GTM, as do other metaphors centring on cognition and the role of the researcher. These also impact on ideas about research and insight more generally.

The metaphors we use influence and direct the ways in which we think about things, with both positive and negative ramifications. Ridding ourselves of using metaphors is not possible; neither is it advisable, since the power of metaphors – by definition, opening up new ways of thinking and imagining – is important, particularly in research approaches aimed at articulating innovative and challenging conceptualizations. *Grounding theory in the data* is a very powerful, illuminating, and innovative metaphor!

The problem with the metaphor encapsulated in the idea that a grounded theory 'emerges' from the data is that it detracts from the active and interpretative nature of research, as researchers seek to move from their data towards credible and coherent forms of abstraction – conceptualizations in the form of theories, models, or frameworks.

For Nietzsche, 'truth is a mobile army of metaphors, metonyms, anthropomorphisms, in short a sum of human relations which have been subjected to poetic and rhetorical intensification, translation and decoration' (quoted in Rorty, 1991, p. 32), a sentiment echoed by Lakoff and Johnson in *Metaphors We Live By* (2003). Researchers and those writing about research methods need to be aware of the role and power of metaphors. The metaphor of *emerging*, a central part of what I have termed 'the GTM mantra' (Bryant, 2017, Chapter 14 and Table 18.1), is double-edged and far too likely to be misleading or ambiguous. If theories are characterized as 'emerging' from the data, then the role of the researcher is somewhat diminished since some level of agency appears to be granted to the data. Even if this is understood and taken into account, it still obscures or detracts from understanding the nature of the role of the researcher(s) as one of being *in dialogue with their data*.

Despite phrases such as 'the theory arises from the data', Glaser and Strauss clearly understood that the relationship between researchers and the data is more complex. Hence, they introduced the term *theoretical sensitivity* in *Discovery* (1967). Kelle (2007, p. 193) has defined this as the 'the ability to *see relevant data* and to reflect upon empirical data material with the help of theoretical terms'. Glaser and Strauss themselves stressed that '[O]nce started, theoretical sensitivity is forever in continual development' (1967, p. 46). They also demonstrated the complex relationship between researchers and their data in their two initial grounded theories – *Awareness* (1965b) and *Time* (1968). Since both were derived from the same data, the theoretical insights for each must have been under the control of the researchers, and reliant on their skills and decisions on how best to pursue one line of thought and leave others for later consideration.

In part, the fault lies with uncritical use of phrases such as 'the theory emerges from the data' and the associated concept of 'emergence' in general. According to the authoritative *Stanford Encyclopedia of Philosophy* (n.d. – entry on emergence), the word 'emergence' is highly problematic.

> Emergence is a notorious philosophical term of art. A variety of theorists have appropriated it for their purposes ever since George Henry Lewes gave it a philosophical sense in his 1875 *Problems of Life and Mind*. We might roughly characterize the shared meaning thus: emergent entities (properties or substances) 'arise' out of more fundamental entities and yet are 'novel' or 'irreducible' with respect to them. (For example, it is sometimes said that consciousness is an emergent property of the brain.) Each of the quoted terms is slippery in its own right, and their specifications yield the varied notions of emergence that we discuss below.

This description certainly resonates with its use in the context of GTM, in the sense that the method is designed to prompt and support researchers moving from the data and the specific context, to higher-level abstractions and concepts which, although clearly derived from the data, encompass properties and explanatory compass that are not reducible to the data itself – i.e. the resulting theory can be said to be an *emergent* entity. But this is not the same as promoting the idea that theories *emerge from* the data. This latter use of the term has too many other potentially misleading and deceptive ramifications and implications, particularly those relating to the role of researchers, the processes of cognition, and generating novel insights.

Similarly, acknowledging that grounded theory is an *emergent* method, in which researchers make methodological decisions through successively studying their data and nascent analyses, does not mean that theory simply arises from the data (Charmaz, 2008a). The process of developing theoretical insights is dependent on researchers examining and analyzing the data, then moving to develop conceptualizations; the initial phase might be understood as a form of induction, but the subsequent stages necessarily involve abduction (see below).

Glaser and Strauss were keen to distinguish GTM from existing methods, particularly those that relied on deriving testable hypotheses from existing theories. They were equally critical of what they termed 'mindless empiricism', evidenced by their reference to Blumer's 'admirable article, addressing himself to the gap between ungrounded theories and the countless empirical studies unguided by any theories' (Glaser & Strauss, 1967, fn, p. 14). Blumer's critique was aimed not only at this 'mindless' approach, but also at the way in which many research projects set out with the objective of producing outcomes that had already been foreshadowed in earlier work (see Bryant, 2017, Chapter 3). Blumer's way of avoiding these contrasting hazards was through recognition of the role of 'sensitizing concepts'. A sensitizing concept

> lacks such specification of attributes or bench marks and consequently it does not enable the user to move directly to the instance and its relevant content. Instead, *it gives the user a general sense of reference and guidance in approaching empirical instances.* (Blumer, 1954, p. 7, emphasis added)

Sensitizing concepts facilitate some forms of investigation but can and do preclude others.

Glaser and Strauss offered a different and starker reaction and resolution to Blumer's criticisms. To avoid the potential for confirmatory bias – setting out to find evidence for what you had already decided was the case – and also to reject what they saw as the somewhat servile and docile deductive model that pervaded US social science, they advocated that doctoral researchers should steer clear of the prevailing and 'authoritative' literature, and so enter the research context with 'as few preconceptions as possible' (Glaser, 1978, pp. 2–3).

Over the years this admonition has taken on a life of its own, so that for many people, including research examiners, journal editors and other gate-keepers, GTM inextricably involves researchers ignoring the relevant literature at the outset, followed by claims along the lines that they undertook their work with no preconceptions or at least somehow circumvented them. A great deal of effort has been expended in correcting such misconceptions, which I regard as 'accidents' rather than as 'essences' of the method (Bryant, 2017, Chapter 4). The rationale for Glaser and Strauss's position in the 1960s is understandable, but we now need to jettison such

advice, which in part derives from the shortcomings of a common metaphor of cognition that is assumed in their writing, and which remains in
Glaser's recent work.

> No preconceived research works as GT. But the worldwide use of GT or sup-
> posed GT versions has increased our knowledge of the subtleties of requiring
> no preconception or giving the arguments for preconceiving research aspects in
> some ways. I hope to detail many of these subtleties in this book *so the reader
> can be aware of what it means to suspend preconceptions in service of emergent
> generating of theory.*
>
> Keep in mind that preconceived concepts do not have to be forgotten. They are
> just to be *suspended* for the GT research so the researcher is open to the emer-
> gent. *Why let them get in the way?* (Glaser, 2012, emphasis added)

Glaser's ideas emanate from 'the conduit metaphor' of communication (see Reddy, 1979; and Bryant, 2006). This metaphor is so common
in everyday parlance that it evades all but the most scrupulous attention – so neither Glaser nor Strauss can be singled out for criticism
on this point. The assumption is that communication operates as a
series of conduits – tubes, channels, ducts – along or through which
information is passed from sender to receiver. Reddy argues that this
representation of communication is highly misleading, since good
communication then appears to resemble friction-free, blockage-free
flow. Consequently, communication problems are characterized as
blockages, breakdowns, or failures between transmission and reception.
Hence Glaser's assertion that preconceived concepts 'get in the way',
implying that effective observation and research is all about clearing a
path of impediments to the development of understanding and insight.

   Glaser also uses the metaphor of 'suspension'; researchers should
'suspend preconceptions'. We may be said to 'suspend' judgement if
we hear differing views about a film or play prior to seeing it for ourselves, but in such cases the options are fairly clear, whereas 'suspending
preconceptions' is a far more complex issue, if indeed it is at all possible.
How do we know what our preconceptions actually are? Preconceptions,
by definition, are often deeply ingrained and taken-for-granted, making
it impossible for anyone to characterize and articulate them as a basis
then for 'suspending' them.

Strauss and Corbin acknowledged that some of the initial GTM texts might have over-played the issue of avoiding existing work, quoting Ian Dey's (1999, p. 251) succinct phrase 'an open mind is not the same as an empty head'. (The phrase is also attributed to Edward Tufte.) But the issue goes further than this, and it requires an understanding of how the conduit metaphor skews the ways in which people talk about and understand cognition. Glaser and Strauss's writings are symptomatic of the idea of cognition as a process requiring a free-flowing path from source to receiver; pre-existing ideas just get in the way. The concomitant assumption is that these existing ideas can be turned off like a tap, allowing researchers to claim either that they have discounted various issues with which they have familiarity, or they are immune to such influences and hold a neutral and disinterested position. Unfortunately, as John Maynard Keynes observed (1936), 'Practical men, who believe themselves to be quite exempt from any intellectual influences, are usually slaves of some defunct economist'. Rather than make claims about suspending, avoiding, or evading preconceptions, it is far better for researchers to explicate and acknowledge the ideas that they hold, and then let others decide the extent to which these influence the process and outcome of the research itself. Those claiming immunity from any such influences, or omitting any reference to them, may well be those most affected by their preconceptions, precisely because they are unaware of them.[2]

In contrast to the conduit metaphor, Reddy (1979, p. 171) proposed what he terms 'the toolmakers' paradigm'. The fundamental difference between the toolmakers' paradigm and the conduit metaphor is that for the latter successful communication appears to be gained without effort, whereas for the former human communication 'will almost always go astray unless real energy is expended' (p. 184). This observation also applies to cognition, where effort is required by all parties to the communication process, and does not incorporate or even allow any passive form of 'reception'. The toolmakers' paradigm aligns with the interpretative/constructivist turn since they share the view that our understanding of reality is a participative, co-constructive, precarious, and continuous project.

Blumer's argument for sensitizing concepts can be understood in this context. Sensitizing concepts do not obstruct our studies and insights but, on the contrary, afford 'a general sense of reference and guidance in approaching empirical instances' (1954, p. 7). Many GTM researchers refer to specific sensitizing concepts, such as feminism, race and ethnicity, and social justice. Some might argue that these concepts have not 'earned their way' in the manner prescribed by Glaser and Strauss. To some extent such suspicions are well founded, particularly if the terms themselves are used in an inept and confirmatory manner. Blumer suggested that:

> hundreds of our concepts – like culture, institutions, social structure, mores, and personality – are not definitive concepts but are sensitizing in nature. They lack precise reference and have no bench marks which allow a clean-cut identification of a specific instance and of its content. Instead, they rest on a general sense of what is relevant. (Blumer, 1954, p. 7)

Sensitizing concepts can be understood as different 'lenses' through which to view research settings; a lens in this context is another metaphor for thinking about cognition. Thus, adding a new lens, or switching one lens out for an alternative, will alter the perspective or orientation from which the context is viewed, much as in an eye-examination by an ophthalmologist. But it is important to take the metaphor further and understand that any 'lens' can also introduce sources of distortion, altered representation, and occlusions. Sensitizing concepts, as enabling mechanisms, allow us to develop our understanding in important ways, and several chapters in *Current Developments* (Bryant & Charmaz, 2019) demonstrate this, using examples such as feminism, culture, injustice, and indigeneity.

In their early GTM texts, particularly *Discovery*, Glaser and Strauss can now be understood to have used the terms 'data', 'theory', and 'concept' largely as sensitizing concepts. They are never defined but play an important role in establishing the basis for GTM. Sensitizing concepts facilitate some forms of investigation but preclude others. In *Discovery*, the argument for GTM was clearly and cogently presented, but, using Blumer's terms, the concept of 'data' lacked 'specification … and consequently [did not] enable the user to move directly to the instance and its relevant content' (Blumer, 1954, p.7). The later critiques of Charmaz and others can then be understood as moving from using 'data' as a sensitizing concept to one where the term becomes subject to detailed and critical examination to see if and how it 'earned its way'. (See below where this is demonstrated at greater length regarding 'theory'.)

Induction and abduction

The 2007 *Handbook* offered new and important insights on the Pragmatist influence on GTM, and the related concept of abduction. GTM continues to be labelled an 'inductive method', but Strauss was already keen to tell people in the 1960s that GTM was an 'abductive method'. Strauss was influenced by Pragmatism throughout his intellectual career, but strangely failed to refer to it explicitly, if at all, in his GTM writings; it is largely relegated to the odd footnote (see Bryant, 2009). On the other hand, GTM among the German-speaking research community was closely associated with Strauss's Pragmatism, and hence also with the issue of abduction. In the 2007 volume, the chapters by Reichertz and Strübing in particular attest to this, and the topic is further developed not only by these contributors, but in other chapters in *Current Developments* (Bryant & Charmaz, 2007a, 2019). GTM writers now cannot ignore the issue, either needing to explain how abduction operates, or to discount it in some manner. For instance, Reichertz (CD:13) provides an argument that concludes starkly that '[T]he logic of Strauss's GT thus permits abductive reasoning, counts on it, enables it, grants it place. More is not necessary.' Many texts, however, continue to claim simply that GTM is 'an inductive method', something that has been taken up by generations of students and other researchers in a largely unexamined manner. (Abduction is an important and complex topic, particularly so for GTM. This section draws on key chapters from both *Handbooks*, also from Bryant (2017, Chapter 13). Readers are advised to go to these sources for further explanation and suggestions for further reading.)

The term 'induction', and various related terms, only occurs a few times in *Discovery*. In Chapter V, Glaser and Strauss (1967, p. 104) refer to grounded theory as 'the constant comparative method', and distinguish it from 'analytic induction' as follows:

> *Analytic induction has been concerned with generating and proving an integrated, limited, precise, universally applicable theory of causes accounting for a specific behavior* (e.g., drug addiction, embezzlement). ... It tests a limited number of hypotheses with all available data, consisting of numbers of clearly defined and carefully selected cases of phenomena. ... The theory is generated by the reformation of hypotheses and redefinition of the phenomena forced by constantly confronting the theory with negative cases, cases which do not confirm the current formulation.

> *In contrast to analytic induction, the constant comparative method is concerned with generating and plausibly suggesting (but not provisionally testing) many categories, properties, and hypotheses about general problems* (e.g., the distribution of services according to the social value of clients). Some of these properties may be causes, as in analytic induction, but unlike analytic induction, others are conditions, consequences, dimensions, types, processes, etc. ... the constant comparisons required by both methods differ in breadth of purpose, extent of comparing, and what data and ideas are compared. (emphasis added)

Kelle (CD:3) offers a helpful note on analytic induction: '[T]heoretical propositions are developed, built and modified through chains of inferences. To obtain a deeper understanding of this process it is important to differentiate between different kinds of theoretical statements with regard to their *scope, source, degree of explicitness* and *empirical content.'*

Hammersley (2004, 2010, 2011) has written extensively on analytic induction and its comparison with GTM. He traces the former through the work of several colleagues and mentors of Strauss, including Becker and Lindesmith, the latter with whom Strauss co-authored an enduring standard text on social psychology (2009).[3] Hammersley argues that Glaser and Strauss were at pains to distinguish between GTM and analytic induction. GTM was a method that used 'explicit coding ... [to] ... serve the function of ... generating and developing theories'. In contrast, analytic induction was

> concerned with generating and proving an integrated, limited, precise, universally applicable theory of causes accounting for a specific behavior (e.g., drug addiction, embezzlement). ... [I]t tests a limited number of hypotheses with *all* available data, consisting of members of clearly defined and carefully selected cases of the phenomena. ... the theory is generated by the reformulation of hypotheses and redefinition of the phenomena **forced** by constantly confronting the theory with negative cases, cases which do not confirm the current formulation. (Hammersley, 2010, italics in original, bold emphasis added)

So most of the discussion on induction in *Discovery* actually refers to something distinct from GTM itself. On the other hand, there is one succinct and unambiguous statement that is the source of part of the GTM mantra.

> In comparing incidents, the analyst learns to see his categories in terms of both their internal development and their changing relations to other categories. For example, as the nurse learns more about the patient, her calculations of social

loss change; and these recalculations change her social loss stories, her loss rationales and her care of the patient.

This is an inductive method of theory development. (Glaser & Strauss, 1967, p. 114, emphasis added)

The problems of induction are well documented and widely discussed (see Bryant, 2017, Chapters 2 and 13), but more pertinently, when considering forms of reasoning, we need to account not only for the logical aspects but also for the cognitive ones. Although Glaser's admonition to avoid 'immaculate conceptualization' is both pithy and relevant in the context of GTM, it ignores the many ways in which researchers develop their insights. Martin (CD:11) quotes Gary Shank's classification of six modes of reasoning:

Shank (1998), for instance, cited six modes that have emerged in the literature, from the type of everyday cognition people utilize to solve problems to empirical research. They are: '(a) reasoning to the reason or hunch; (b) reasoning to the clue; (c) reasoning to the metaphor or analogy; (d) reasoning to the symptom; (e) reasoning to the pattern; (f) reasoning to the explanation' (Shank, 1998, pp. 848–849).

The categorization is derived from Shank's work, based on his reformulation of Peirce's 'ten classes of signs' in the context of his (Shank's) consideration of Peirce's work on semiotics and abduction.[4] In the paper co-authored with Cunningham (1996) they move from 'categorization' to consideration of 'inference', asking 'what can the ten classes tell us about *how human beings reason and make inferences about their world?*' (emphasis added). Although they do not spell out the ramifications here, elsewhere Shank (1998) has stressed that his aim is to demonstrate that abduction is as much a 'psychological concept' as a 'logical and semiotic' one. As Reichertz argues both in the 2007 volume and *Current Developments* (CD:13), it is critical to maintain and defend the understanding of abduction as both logical and cognitive. He quotes Peirce to the effect that abduction 'takes place "like lightning", and the thought process "is *very little hampered* by logical rules"' (emphasis added). Making inferences is an embodied cognitive process, encompassing a logical form of reasoning, but also involving something along the lines of what Glaser and Strauss termed 'theoretical sensitivity'.

Charmaz has characterized abduction as 'a type of reasoning that begins by examining data and after scrutiny of these data, and defining an unusual finding, *entertains all possible explanations for this data*, and then forms hypotheses to confirm or disconfirm until the researcher arrives at the most plausible interpretation of the observed data' (Charmaz, 2014a, emphasis added). This begs the question 'plausible for whom?'. Initially this will be the researcher(s) themselves, and any advisors or evaluators; later the plausibility of the interpretation should be judged more widely, although, as Glaser and Strauss argued, a grounded theory, and indeed other theories, are often proven to be of 'great practical use long before the theory is tested with great rigor' (*Awareness*, 1965b, p. 293).

Explaining the role of abduction in GTM makes the method more understandable and plausible. Reichertz has described Peirce's concept of abduction as involving an 'out-manoeuvring' of one's existing knowledge and expectations; an alternative metaphor to that of suspending or abandoning one's preconceptions. He also argues that the divergence between Glaser and Strauss in their later writings can best be understood as oriented around the idea of abduction: Strauss takes it up and uses it to distance his idea of the method, not only from deductive methods of investigation but also from being simply 'inductive'. The stress is on generating new ideas and concepts. Glaser, on the other hand, adheres to the centrality of induction and theory emerging from the data.

Reichertz offers a clear and succinct distinction between deduction, induction, and abduction. In stark terms, he states that deduction is tautological but 'truth-conveying', while qualitative induction is tautological but 'not truth-conveying'. What he refers to as 'qualitative induction' is

> not a valid but only a probable form of inference, although it does have the advantage of being capable of operationalization (albeit with difficulty). Qualitative induction is the basis of all scientific procedures that find, in collected data, only new versions of what is already known. (Reichertz, CD:13)

Hence his conclusion that GTM cannot lead to new theoretical insights if it is purely and simply inductive.

In contrast to qualitative induction, Reichertz refers to procedures that lead to 'an abductive discovered order'. An outcome that is primarily a 'mental construct' since 'the search for order is never definitively complete and is always undertaken provisionally'. This is bound up with his stress on abduction as primarily and ineluctably a cognitive process. These constructs or hypotheses must then be amenable to a 'multi-stage process of checking'.

> Abductive inferencing does not double the amount of data but *construes* a concept, an idea, a theory which makes the action the data represent comprehensible and explains it. Research that takes an abductive approach makes action comprehensible by indicating the regularities this action is based on, making its motives apparent, to an extent far beyond what the acting individuals themselves are aware of. (Reichertz, CD:13, original emphasis)

It is important to understand that when Reichertz refers to a multi-stage process of checking he is not advocating some form of positivist or empiricist verification. His primary claim is that any theory has to be comprehensible and plausible, again prompting the response 'comprehensible and plausible to whom?', but anchoring the issue in the realm of a Pragmatist view of knowledge, not a positivist/empiricist one. Theories are to be justified primarily in terms of their 'usefulness', and hypotheses judged in terms of consistency, coherence, credibility, and rigour. Knowledge claims require and rely on cognitive and social foundations, or in Rorty's stark terms: 'Truth is what your contemporaries allow you to get away with'.[5]

Reichertz's chapter in 2007 stressed the cognitive nature of abduction. It is not something that can be automated, despite the claims of those in the AI (artificial intelligence) community who argue otherwise. He noted ironically that '[T]he great success of abduction, in my opinion, may be traced back to two particular features: first to its *indefiniteness* and second to the *misjudgment of the achievements* of abduction that derive from this' (2007, p. 216, emphasis added). He repeats this in his new chapter (CD:13), explaining that abduction has been mis-characterized as a 'rule-governed way to new knowledge', and taken up by those looking for a logical basis for something that might become machine-based.

He also, quite correctly, distinguishes between serendipity and abduction. Abduction 'brings a novel idea into the world', but, unlike serendipity, it does not rely on luck. On the other hand, the concept of 'theoretical sensitivity' brings the two together much along the lines of Louis Pasteur's point that 'in the fields of observation chance favours *only* the prepared mind'. (NB: The word 'only' is often omitted when people use this aphorism.) These aspects can coincide, for instance, in Benoit Mandelbrot's account of how his ideas about 'fractals' and 'roughness' came about.[6]

Mandelbrot wondered how things might have turned out differently had someone cleaned the blackboard before he entered the room. He refers to Pasteur's
maxim to the effect that chance favors the prepared mind, but adds that 'I also
think that my long string of lucky breaks can be credited to *my mode of paying
attention:* I look at funny things and *never hesitate to ask questions*' (emphasis
added). This outlook gives encouragement to the sorts of *abductive* leaps that
involve 'pattern recognition', but it also emphasizes that such insights require a
basis in prior experience or expertise. (Bryant, 2017, Chapter 16, p. 321)

An abductive understanding of GTM, and more generally an appreciation
of abduction itself, acquires plausibility and credibility since it also resonates with key writings on the ways in which we understand the world and
reflect on our experience and knowledge. For instance, Michael Polanyi,
in *Personal Knowledge* (1958) and *The Tacit Dimension* (1966), argued essentially that 'we can know more than we can tell'. A maxim taken up by
Donald Schön, who refers to Geoffrey Vickers to the effect that 'in all our
ordinary judgments of quality, we "can recognize and describe deviations
from a norm very much more clearly than we [can] describe the norm
itself"' (Schön, 1983, p. 53). This all resonates with the idea quoted above
from *Discovery*, that a grounded theory can be practically useful long before
it receives wider theoretical affirmation.

Taken together this provides the basis for the realization that although
some aspects of our activities and practices can be described in terms of
rules and procedures, there are other complexities that cannot. Schön
(1983) argues that there has to be an understanding that

> [W]hen we go about the spontaneous, intuitive performance of the actions
> of everyday life, we show ourselves *to be knowledgeable in a special way.*
> Often, we cannot say what we know. When we try to describe it, we find
> ourselves at a loss, or we produce descriptions that are obviously inappropri-
> ate. Our knowing is ordinarily tacit, implicit in our patterns of action and in
> our feel for the stuff with which we are dealing. It seems right to say that our
> knowing is in our action. And similarly, the workaday life of the professional
> practitioner reveals, in its recognitions, judgments and skills, a pattern of
> tacit knowing-in-action. (1983, p. 49, emphasis added)

It is critical to understand that abduction, far from being something
strange and alien is to a limited extent a process common to all of us. We
are all proficient and expert in a range of activities that at one time or
another were very new to us but are now part of our general repertoire;
for instance, riding a bike, driving a car, playing a musical instrument, or

making a cup of tea. Mostly we accomplish these tasks intuitively and almost automatically; we do not have to think about each aspect or action. But if something unusual occurs, we find ourselves confronted by a level of uncertainty that may force us to attend to detailed aspects of our behaviour that in the normal course of events remain implicit or taken for granted.

In other words, we become abductive, taking leaps in our reasoning, often because to delay would lead to failure or disaster – e.g. if the car we are driving starts to skid, or the brakes fail on our bicycle. Schön refers to this as 'reflecting in action' as opposed to 'reflecting on action'. The former happens quickly and leads immediately to response or action, the latter is more considered, and involves thinking about something that happened in the past and assessing how it could have been done differently or more effectively. Reflecting in action opens up the possibilities of seeing things in a new light, casting off the habits and assumptions that usually sustain our actions. If this is followed later on by reflecting on these new possibilities, it may result in fresh insights and ideas that can be tested more rigorously.

In the context of *doing research*, the necessity to respond quickly and immediately is not normally a requirement. But developing new insights, and breaking away from ingrained assumptions and patterns of thinking, does not come easily or naturally, particularly if the research objective is to test what is already accepted as part of the theoretical canon. This difficulty is exacerbated if researchers are expected to serve an apprenticeship that involves close study of the classic theories – the received wisdom.

Glaser and Strauss sought to circumvent this problem in part by developing a method of research that was designed to maximize the chances of encountering uncertainty and surprise, thereby encouraging development of new conceptual insights and theories. Hence 'out-manoeuvring' our existing knowledge, as Reichertz contends. Close encounters with research contexts and 'data' parallel to some extent the wide range of experiences that practitioners will encounter in the course of their daily activities. Inevitably, some of these will produce surprises, the responses to which may well result in innovative insights and reconsideration of people's received understanding of domain knowledge. By intervening in the research setting and encouraging participants to think about aspects of their activities and environment that are usually taken for granted, GTM elicits features that otherwise might go unnoticed. In some cases, this process might become evident as the data is being gathered, but it also might only come to light at a later stage when the data is being scrutinized and reflected on in memos.

This all provides the basis for a more cogent explanation of the ways in which innovative insights arise, and the role of specific methods in facilitating this. Peirce himself argued that abduction was aided either by 'fear' or 'musement'. One or other may be beneficial, but they are not sufficient. If abductive leaps are to be given a more robust and rigorous basis, something further has to be incorporated, very much along the lines of the later stages of GTM, particularly theoretical coding and theoretical saturation.

Abduction is now far more clearly and cogently understood to be an essential feature of GTM than was the case in 2007. Reichertz (CD:13) sums up the position succinctly:

> The question whether GT (in the variant of Strauss and the early Strauss and Corbin) contains an abductive research logic can therefore be answered with a resounding 'yes'. Fortunately, however, it does not only contain the logic of abductive reasoning but also that of qualitative induction. The logic of Strauss's GT thus permits abductive reasoning, counts on it, enables it, grants it place. More is not necessary.

Now that the abductive nature of GTM has become more fully articulated, it can be seen as the leading method for *enacting abstraction and abduction*.

GTM and abduction – some alternative and *elementary* viewpoints

In contrast to Reichertz, Tavory and Timmermans (CD:26) now argue that 'abductive analysis' is distinct from GTM since each approach asks different types of question. Their chapter makes a number of important points regarding the paucity of work that takes and builds upon an initially substantive grounded theory and develops a formal one, or develops the key conceptualizations in some other manner. But they largely build upon an incomplete view of GTM and fail to account for the ways in which the method has been developed and enhanced. Some aspects of their critique do apply, however, across research methods generally.[7]

Interestingly, they group abductive analysis with the extended case method (ECM), and analytic induction. The former was developed by Burawoy (1998) as part of his criticism of Glaser and Strauss's original statement of GTM.[8] Analytic induction has already been referred to since it was specifically discussed in *Discovery* as a contrasting approach to GTM.

For Tavory and Timmermans, abductive analysis, ECM, and analytic induction share a concern with the same 'central question' and the objective of 'explicitly ... connecting observations with existing bodies of theory'. They argue that this makes them all distinct from GTM. This contention can be criticized on several counts. The first is that this ignores the way in which GTM incorporates abduction – or abductive analysis – *as a technique* within GTM; now widely recognized as a method that incorporates and encourages abduction understood as a form of cognitive-cum-logical inference. Reichertz (CD:13) states this succinctly: 'GT thus permits abductive reasoning, counts on it, enables it, grants it place. More is not necessary.' I would affirm this, stating that GTM *enacts abstraction and abduction* at its core.

Second, Tavory and Timmermans appear to rely on a version of GTM that includes several non-essential aspects of the method. For instance, they refer to axial coding, which they contrast with 'abductive analysis', even though the former, introduced by Strauss and Corbin (1990 & 1998), is not an essential aspect of GTM and has been roundly criticized by diverse grounded theorists, including, separately, Charmaz and Glaser. Tavory and Timmermans also mention *in vivo* codes, which they argue have 'been relatively popular in grounded theory circles', but again the GTM literature is replete with caveats about reliance on such data in subsequent conceptualization.

The third criticism derives from their identification of the common objective shared by abductive analysis, ECM, and analytic induction – i.e. 'explicitly ... connecting observations with existing bodies of theory' – and their view that this is not part of GTM. They support the GTM-based admonition 'against researchers imposing stock theoretical ideas on their research materials', but then claim that '*coding without constantly referring to theoretical anticipations* may have created the opposite problem: *a collection of thinly abstracted analyses unmoored in our community of inquiry*' (emphasis added). Yet GTM explicitly incorporates engaging with the relevant 'community of inquiry' as an aspect of 'theoretical coding', aimed at weaving 'the fractured story back together again (Glaser, 1978, p. 72) into "an organized whole theory (Glaser, 1998, p. 163)"' (quoted by Hernandez, 2009). Recent PhD student accounts (e.g. Bryant, 2017, Chapter 19) illustrate this process, demonstrating how these skills can be honed, leading to theoretical and conceptual articulations incorporating researchers *going to* and *engaging with* the literature for support and positioning at appropriate stages of their work; something that is often critical at several points in a researcher's stages of analysis. This combination of both theoretical and methodological sensitivity is a core aspect of GTM as it has developed in the past 50 years.

In a further contrast to GTM, Tavory and Timmermans claim that abductive analysis has 'a distinct *realist dimension*: not anything goes, the researcher cannot wish analytical categories into existence'. Although I doubt that they mean to imply that for GTM 'anything goes', their argument might be misunderstood in this sense. More critically, they offer a misplaced defence of realism, and so repeat the fallacies of writers such as Sartwell (2015), who misconstrue the Pragmatist position of Dewey and, more recently, Rorty (see Bryant, 2017, Chapter 17).

It is worth dwelling on Sartwell's fallacy in order to dispel any misunderstanding. Sartwell argues, contra Rorty, that:

> recent work in philosophy includes various forms of realism about the world: *the idea that reality is not the product of consciousness*, or of human perceptual structures or languages or interpretive communities, but exists independently. We don't make the world, as one might put it; the world makes us. (Sartwell, 2015, emphasis added?)

In essence, he is accusing Rorty of arguing that 'reality is the *product of consciousness*'. This is absurd. In fact, it is such poor thinking that 'it is not even wrong' – a phrase coined by the physicist Wolfgang Pauli when commenting on work that was especially ill-conceived. In *Contingency, Irony, and Solidarity* (1989), perhaps his most important book, Rorty explicitly argues that:

> Truth cannot be out there – cannot exist independently of the human mind – because sentences cannot so exist, or be out there. *The world is out there, but descriptions of the world are not.* Only descriptions of the world can be true or false. The world on its own unaided by the describing activities of humans cannot. (Rorty, 1989, p. 4, emphasis added)[9]

Rorty never denied the existence of reality, but he did deny the possibility of humans accessing or discussing reality in any non-linguistic fashion.

Tavory and Timmermans correctly view abduction as an important technique for generating novel insights, and they seek to offer a useful characterization of what is involved. But in so doing they go too far in distancing it from GTM, which I and many others would argue is potentially one of the most effective methods for facilitating and fostering abduction as part of the research process.

Is abduction *elementary*?

Many writers on GTM refer to Sherlock Holmes, although not always in the same manner. Strübing has noted that when Strauss worked in Chicago with Goffman, Davis, Shibutani, Freidson, and Becker, they formed themselves into a group called 'The Chicago School Irregulars', deliberately evoking the 'Baker Street Irregulars' in the Sherlock Holmes stories. Strauss's group was dedicated to 'studying natural settings, daily life, everyday worlds, social worlds and urban lifestyles...' (Lofland, 1980; see also Strübing, 2007, p.19). But Strübing now doubts the veracity of this, and does not refer to it in his current chapter.

Flick (CD:6), discussing abduction, quotes from Kennedy and Thornberg that '[L]ike the fictional detective Sherlock Holmes, [abductive researchers] constantly move back and forth between data and theories, and make comparisons and interpretations in searching for patterns and the best possible explanations (Kennedy & Thornberg, 2018, p. 52)'. In contrast, Thornberg and Dunne (CD:10) argue that Glaser and Strauss criticized Merton, because '[L]ike the fictive detective Sherlock Holmes [Merton's] reasoning necessarily leads to the position *that data should fit the theory*, in contrast to our position that *the theory should fit the data*' (Glaser & Strauss, 1967, p. 261). So is Sherlock Holmes an example of an expert in abduction or not? I would argue that Holmes does employ a specific form of abduction.

Although Conan Doyle and Peirce were contemporaries, they lived in different countries and it is highly unlikely that either one was aware of the other's work. If anything, it is more likely that Peirce would have known about Sherlock Holmes, than would Conan Doyle have heard about, let alone read, any of Peirce's writings. So it is not surprising that Holmes' logical processes are referred to as 'deductive' rather than abductive; but abductive they certainly are. Albeit, Conan Doyle describes Holmes' thought processes in a slightly different way to more conventional ideas about abduction – i.e. 'Once you eliminate the impossible, whatever remains, no matter how improbable, must be the truth'. This draws attention to the process of eliminating possibilities, then engaging in further investigation of what remains, with the aim of clarifying the most plausible explanation.[10] Sherlock Holmes explained this form of reasoning to his amanuensis, claiming that 'it is elementary my dear Watson'.

But for Dr Watson it was far from 'elementary'. Whenever he tried to copy Holmes' methods he failed miserably. Similarly, with abduction; the outcomes of abductive processes can and should have what Charmaz terms 'credibility' and 'resonance' for others apart from the researcher(s) themselves, but this is not to imply that anyone can become an adept, nor that abduction is some natural talent. It takes determination, practice, and experience, and GTM offers a well-founded path for developing and applying these skills.

Stories, narratives, and fairy-tales

In an earlier article, Tavory and Timmermans (2009) contrasted GTM with Burawoy's ECM, seeing the former as using 'ethno-narratives' developed from 'actors in the field', and ECM as relying on 'theoretical narratives'. They see narrativity as entirely misplaced in sociological research, since it enforces closure and finality. 'The narrative is in essence a fable – seductive exactly because it is alien to the very structure of the historical world, supplying it with the false coherence and solidity that we crave' (Tavory & Timmermans, 2009, p. 249). In their chapter (CD:26), they refer to the way 'the researcher looks for what's *the story* in the empirical materials' (emphasis added). They see the ethno-narratives of GTM as 'a naïve, artificial closure *grounded* in social life and disregarding the researcher's role in theoretically circumscribing the events' (2009, p. 249).

Again, their criticisms have some cogency, but are critically incomplete. Imposing a single narrative, with closure and finality, is certainly not an effective research strategy. But there is rarely just one version of the narrative; hence the *Rashomon* effect. The term derives from the film *Rashomon*, in which a murder is described by four witnesses in four entirely contradictory ways. *The Simpsons* offers a powerful and succinct summation.

Marge: Come on, Homer. Japan will be fun! You liked *Rashomon*.
Homer: That's not how I remember it![11]

Narrative does have a place in GTM, but it needs to be understood against a context of the *Rashomon* effect and the role of abduction. Birks and Mills (CD:12) discuss the storyline approach, defining it as 'as an advanced analytical technique used in grounded theory research for the purpose of both integrating and articulating theory'. It allows a grounded theory to be 'rendered and articulated', encompassing the three dimensions of the 'narrative turn' – i.e. 'interaction, continuity and situation, each of which are pertinent for a grounded theory analysis'. This approach is not new to GTM, and Charmaz points out that Strauss always emphasized finding the analytic story in the data, as David Hayes-Bautista, an early graduate of UCSF recalled (Charmaz, 2000). Birks and Mills (CD:12) explain that:

> [T]he first and most extensive reference to storyline was made by Strauss and Corbin in their initial *Basics of Qualitative Research* text (Strauss & Corbin, 1990). In this text, storyline was defined as 'the *conceptualization of the story'* (p. 116) as part of the selective coding process. In developing the storyline, these authors assert that the researcher moves from descriptive to analytical telling of the story evident in the data. *Through presenting the storyline as a mechanism for moving the research from description to conceptualization*, Strauss and Corbin (1990) make a significant contribution to grounded theory. (emphasis added)

Dey (2007) similarly argues that narrative can be an effective way of bringing the temporal and structural elements to the fore. But this will also demand theoretical sensitivity from the researcher(s), who will need to employ abduction in moving the narrative from description to conceptualization, in a manner precisely akin to that singled out for commendation by Wacquant (see above). Moreover, by understanding and taking account of the *Rashomon* effect, GTM researchers can evade the sort of criticism voiced by Burawoy (1991), who argued that Grounded Theorists, in claiming to let the data simply speak for itself, are simply supporting the status quo, and leaving things as they are. They can allow and present alternative narratives, examining each one, then justifying their choice of which one(s) to take forward to conceptualization, eliminating the 'impossible' while developing the 'most plausible'.

Notes

1 Dickens, *Hard Times*, p. 3, online edition available at www.gutenberg.org/files/786/786-h/786-h.htm.
2 Charmaz (2014a, 2017b) observes that grounded theory prescriptions to abandon or suspend preconceptions address ideas from extant theory and research, not the more fundamental preconceptions on which researchers base their taken-for-granted identities. She argues that these preconceptions can shape or saturate the researcher's views of the data and subsequent analysis.
3 An 8th edition appeared in 1999 edited by Lindesmith, Strauss, and Denzin.
4 Kathy has pointed out that Shank (1987, 1998) has long advocated using abduction and has an appreciative audience among critical psychologists (see, for example, Stainton-Rogers, 2003).

5 This quote is attributed to Rorty, and he almost certainly used it in lectures and seminars. The published version is as follows: 'I can sum up what I have been saying about appeals to experience as follows: experience gives us no way to drive a wedge between the cultural–political question of what we should talk about and the question of what really exists. For what counts as an accurate report of experience is a matter of what a community will let you get away with.' (2007, p. 11)

6 See www.edge.org/3rd_culture/obrist10/obrist10_index.html

7 Tavory and Timmermans, referring to the ways in which debates about 'theorization and evidence ... may have been unnecessarily adversarial', assert that 'a sub-discipline needs to be quite confident about its place to go after its own'. But the contrary would seem to be the case. The compulsion to criticize alternatives usually springs from lack of confidence, and the potential for one's own position to be misconstrued and identified too closely with one or more of the alternatives that are then confronted. Glaser and Strauss's use of various terms to distinguish GTM from other approaches derives from this latter, somewhat precarious position, rather than the former, more confident one – see below.

8 Although many sociologists claim adherence to ECM, particularly in the form of Burawoy's 'public sociology', the extent of its use pales against that of GTM.

9 Errol Morris (See Chapter 2, p. 56, note 4) is clearly in the same camp as Sartwell, http://bostonreview.net/politics/errol-morris-there-such-thing-truth

10 In my article on Strauss's failure to mention Pragmatism in his GTM writings I referred to 'The Adventure of Silver Blaze' in which Holmes notes the 'curious incident of the dog in the night-time' – the curious thing being that the dog did nothing in the night-time. See Bryant, 2009.

11 http://whatculture.com/tv/10-incredibly-subtle-jokes-simpsons-might-missed?page=3

4

GTM PARADOXES

In 2007 (Bryant & Charmaz, 2007b), we discussed some paradoxical aspects of GTM, something that is still all too evident in the literature. For instance, some writers claim that GTM is easy and comes naturally, but then go on to argue that not everyone can conceptualize. In a sense, such contradictory statements are understandable and explicable given that GTM is a method specifically aimed at novice and inexperienced researchers, providing them with guidelines that offer a basis for overcoming any lack of confidence in putting forward and developing their own theoretical insights. As such it is crucial that obstacles and impediments are dismantled and defused, but not disregarded. So encouraging researchers needs to be tempered with an understanding that the process of conceptualizing requires skill and exper- tise, and no one can rely on 'natural ability'. This is expressed succinctly as 'the more I practice the luckier I get', attributed both to renowned golfers Arnold Palmer and Gary Player. The GTM version might be something like: 'The more I undertake GTM research, the easier I find it to develop persua- sive and credible conceptualizations.' Clearly, this acknowledges the active role played by researchers in the process.

GTM and sociology

In addition to the paradoxes and perplexities we noted in 2007 (Bryant & Charmaz, 2007a), there is also the issue of the relationship between GTM and sociology. *Discovery* was written as a challenge to the US social science orthodoxy of the time. Strauss himself was a key figure in the Chicago School, itself something of a maverick academy. Glaser, although influenced by Lazarsfeld, was never an established member of Columbia University. All of this may explain why the relationship between GTM and sociology is complex and peculiar. In discussing Glaser's Basic Social Processes, Kelle (CD:3) argues that: '[T]he emergence of theoretical codes or categories from the data is dependent on the ability to grasp empirical phenomena in theoretical terms, or, in other words, on "theoretical sensitivity", *a competence that demands training and background in sociological theory* (which Glaser also still conceded, see Glaser, 1992, p. 28)' (emphasis added). Similarly, Morse and Clark (CD:7) refer to the 'sociological primacy' of GTM, and Tavory and Timmermans (CD:26) state that GTM 'presumes empirical observations are inherently sociologically relevant'.

In practice, however, many GTM-oriented researchers make little or no use of sociological theories. Moreover, within sociology the writings of Glaser and Strauss, and other GTM resources, have nothing like the recognition that they have elsewhere. Martin (CD:11) argues that 'I concur with Gibson and Hartman's (2014) observation that *the lack of engagement with sociology hampers grounded theories*' (emphasis added). This may, of course, be a result of the ways in which many GTM researchers articulate their outcomes against a wide variety of theoretical resources that go above and beyond the ones they might have expected in the earliest stages of their research.

I would argue that it is precisely the transdisciplinary nature of much GTM research that affords the 'grab' and 'fit' of grounded theories, conceptualized against the relevant theoretical context deemed most applicable once theoretical coding takes place. In Charmaz's terms: credibility, originality, resonance, and usefulness (Charmaz, 2006, 2014a). Other research methods may also lead to such outcomes, but GTM specifically advocates these aspects as prime objectives and criteria of quality. Again, as Glaser and Strauss stated in *Awareness*, grounded theories are often shown to have 'great practical use long before [they are] tested with great rigor' (Glaser & Strauss, 1965b, p. 293).

Clarke (CD:1) offers one perspective on how sociology developed from the 1950s, locating GTM against this and going on to argue that *Situational Analysis* (SA) is one component of what she terms 'the (re)turn to the social'. This move has

coalesced around a number of often overlapping or hybrid approaches. In qualitative inquiry across the disciplines these currently include: Bourdieusian field theory, Foucauldian discourse analysis, Foucauldian *dispositif* or apparatus, actor-network theory (ANT), assemblage theory, rhizomic analytics, and the hybrid method of SA. All have earlier roots but have been varyingly renovated to take recent developments into fuller account. (NB: Clarke explains all these terms in her chapter.)

SA, in particular, 'relies on the inherent strength of constructivist GT in closely attending to context by "turning away from acontextual description" (Charmaz 2006: 271). In fact, in SA, I explicitly drew upon the concept of *situation* instead of context (Clarke 2005: 71–72)'.

Previously I briefly referred to Irwin's belief that recent developments around GTM have demonstrated its important contribution to the ways in which sociologists try to link structure and agency. Similarly, Duckles et al. (CD:31) draw attention to Charmaz's (2014a) contention that GTM, through its links to Symbolic Interactionism, not only encompasses processes and meaning-making at the micro level of interactions, but also addresses macro processes of change, emergence, agency, and negotiated order. Similarly, Strübing credits Strauss with having 'steered interactionism into the position of a full-fledged empirically-oriented sociology encompassing micro, meso, and macro level issues'. This incorporates Strauss's non-GTM writings with GTM itself, particularly his final book *Continual Permutations of Action* (Strauss, 1993). So it is surprising that GTM is often held at arm's length by sociologists, exemplified in the previous discussion on Wacquant, albeit that he was writing more than 15 years ago, before Charmaz published *Constructing Grounded Theory* (2006), but well after her earlier constructivist GTM writings.

A further curious and noteworthy example is provided by Manuel Castells, who refers to his developing a 'grounded theory of power' in *Communication Power* (2009, p. 5). The list of references lacks any from Glaser, Strauss, or any other GTM text. Later, in his article 'A sociology of power: My intellectual journey', he refers to 'the quest for a grounded theory of power', 'the embrace of grounded theory as a strategy of theory building', and 'my deliberate option to engage in grounded theory rather than in grand theory' (Castells, 2016, pp. 1, 4, 4). Again, there are no references to any GTM literature, and Castells describes his approach as follows: 'I would start with theoretical constructs but always use them as research tools to be modified and systematized only in terms of their usefulness in the process of discovery' (2016, p. 4). Which is not in any way a helpful, or indeed accurate or informed, summary of GTM!

The examples of Wacquant and Castells are indicative of the perplexing relationship between GTM and sociology, and I leave it to others to decide how to apportion responsibility. More critically, the GTM community need to take it on themselves to remedy the situation, to the benefit of all concerned. It would certainly seem to be the case that many GTM-oriented researchers – and researchers in general – would benefit from a clearer understanding of what is involved in 'thinking sociologically'. A good place to begin would be Zygmunt Bauman's book of that title (Bauman & May, 2001). Conversely, sociologists and others in related disciplines with a paucity of understanding of GTM, similar to that of the two eminent theorists already referred to, would do well to refrain from ill-informed criticism and misuse of the GTM label. They should at the very least develop an understanding of the method, referring to key GTM sources and reflecting on the ways in which GTM might influence their own work and discipline in general. As Strübing (CD:2) suggests, Strauss's concepts of 'arenas' and 'social worlds' would be a good starting point.

A strange hostility

Related to all of this is a further and enduring paradox of GTM. Despite its obvious popularity and widespread use, often leading to significant developments in practice, GTM continues to be regarded with suspicion or even hostility by many gate-keepers – research evaluators, Institutional Review Boards (IRBs) or their equivalent, examiners, editors, and reviewers – partly due to the sort of ill-informed views of GTM exemplified above.

There are indeed many examples of 'poor GTM research', both in terms of the research itself being poorly conceived and carried out, and in terms of the ways in which GTM has been used/misused. But this is common across all forms of research and all methods. For a variety of reasons, what I have termed 'methodologizing' often incorporates a form of branding, and researchers and evaluators expect research reports to indicate the chosen method – or *brand* – clearly and succinctly. The result is that claims by researchers with regard to methods are often specious or misleading. In the 1990s Strauss and Corbin (1994) worried about GTM becoming 'fashionable', anticipating the downside of 'methodological consumerism' (Crossman & Noma, CD:29), which also resonates with Mruck and Mey (CD:23), who refer to the use of GTM as a 'legitimizing label'; although for some it is a de-legitimizing one.

Strauss and Corbin also worried that GTM would become 'old hat', but that is certainly not the case. Indeed, given the popularity of GTM, the number of examples of poor GTM research, and misuse of the legitimizing label, is hardly surprising, but again a thorough and grounded study of methods-in-use – across methods generally – might transform what are largely anecdotal claims into more rigorous and credible ones. Researchers using GTM, in whatever form or combination, do, however, need to pre-empt the main criticisms levelled at the method, offering clear statements with regard to the rationale for their research, the processes and procedures that they have followed or intend to undertake, clearly explaining the ways in which their analysis evolves, and providing the basis for their insights (Bryant, 2017, Chapter 18, especially Tables 18.2 and 18.3).

Over the years I have given an introductory seminar on GTM with the title 'The Grounded Theory Method: A Model of Good Research Practice'. But I begin by examining the all-too-common view of GTM as a model of bad practice that seems to allow – if not actually encourage – inadequacies such as failing to clarify the initial research question, disregarding the literature, and engaging with the problem domain without a clear strategy. All of which leads to consideration of how GTM relates to and sheds light on general issues of research practice, dismantling and rebutting the all-too-common misunderstandings upon which this image of GTM as bad practice is predicated.

GTM and researching in general

As I noted earlier, Martin (CD:11) refers to Flick (2015), who

> observed that many of the challenges that faced qualitative research in the 1980s and 1990s, including concerns with rigor and quality, remain. He also summarized a number of emerging concerns internationally. He identified trends such as evidence-based research and the rise of big social science projects, with collaborators across departments and institutions, as a threat to small, individual qualitative studies.

Rather than seeing this as some palpable failing across the whole qualitative endeavour, I believe that continuing concerns with rigour, quality, and practical relevance should be understood as inevitable aspects of research and the yearning for enhanced knowledge and understanding, based on recognition that these are all subject to ambivalence and contingency.

Those gate-keepers who disparage specific methods – GTM being a common target – should cast their nets more widely, paying more attention to the products of research and less to any idiosyncratic preconceptions about particular approaches. Moreover, GTM itself has two key features that are often seen as weaknesses, but in fact need to be understood as sources of strength incorporating aspects of research that should be understood and implemented more generally.

The first is the issue of *theoretical saturation*, which is widely misunderstood and often claimed by researchers with little or no justification. All research involves a compromise in deciding when to end a project and report on the results. Theoretical saturation provides a clear focus on which to base any such decision; something that many other methods fail to address. Understood correctly, theoretical saturation requires researchers to explain the basis for bringing their data gathering and analysis to an end, moving on to report their findings and present their conclusions. This form of saturation can be claimed when researcher(s) can justify that there is sufficient data to substantiate their model – i.e. that the categories in their model are borne out by the data, and that further data drawn from their research context adds no further detail to the categories and concepts already articulated. But the basis for such claims is widely misunderstood and misused, and researchers often assert that investigation of the research context has provided 'no further data' or 'no new data', sometimes referring to this simply as 'saturation' or even 'data saturation'. This is wildly inaccurate and does disservice to GTM.

Glaser and Strauss offered a clear definition of the term in *Discovery*: '[Theoretical] Saturation means that no additional data are being found whereby the sociologist can *develop properties of the category*' (1967, p. 61, emphasis added). This can be incorporated into other research methods as part of 'good practice'. Charmaz correctly notes that theoretical sampling and the progression from this to theoretical saturation go well beyond the idea of GTM as purely inductive. 'It involves a form of reasoning, abduction, *which distinguishes grounded theory*' (Charmaz, 2014a, p. 200, emphasis added).

The other aspect worthy of attention in this context is *theoretical coding*. Kelle (CD:3) defines this as one way that GTM advocates

> a non-deductive use of theories and models in the process of empirically grounded theory building. Thereby a variety of new and complex concepts were proposed like 'theoretical coding', 'coding families', 'axial coding', 'coding paradigm' and many others.

Many now see Glaser's coding families, and Strauss and Corbin's coding paradigm as equivalent, offering paths from codes and categories to concise and integrated theoretical statements. On the other hand, my experience with numerous PhD students indicates that in many cases neither is necessary; indeed, each has drawbacks that can mislead students. Doctoral students seem to be able to move to a point where they can combine the outcomes of their focused coding with theoretical coding, and relate categories to one another, indicating 'possible relationships' (Charmaz), that 'weave the fractured story back together' (Glaser), cogently presenting their findings. This is often accomplished with a *return to* and *engagement with* the literature once the conceptual model has been developed from the data. This constitutes a key component of theoretical coding, and the literature deemed relevant to this stage of 'constant comparison' is often largely or completely different from the literature investigated at the earliest stages of the research. This is commonplace for GTM research, and most, if not all, PhD students when asked 'what surprised you in your research?' are readily able to respond with clear aspects of their findings that proved unexpected and could not have been predicted at the outset.

As was pointed out earlier, Wacquant, in praising Duneier's work, described it in terms that resonate with the process of theoretical coding, even if neither he nor Duneier seem to have understood it as such. Castells similarly hints at his use of existing theories, albeit exhibiting limited understanding of the process and GTM in general.

This key aspect of GTM is often ignored or misunderstood, leading to unfounded criticisms of the method. In 1994, Strauss and Corbin noted that in far too many cases researchers were claiming use of GTM but failing to accomplish more than a fairly mundane level of coding, certainly not moving on to theoretical coding, then generating theoretical statements. As a result, they noted that the complaint 'where is the theory in grounded theory' was invoked in methodological critiques or texts. This invocation has not disappeared (see below).

The theory in grounded theory

One apparent enigma of GTM is the paucity of substantive and formal grounded theories (SGTs and FGTs) more than 50 years after the method and the first grounded theory made an appearance. Several of the chapters in *Current Developments* (Bryant & Charmaz, 2019) consider the ways in which 'theory' is understood, both generally, and specifically in the context of GTM. Without wishing to pre-empt these discussions, I take up some of these issues below, but note that good theories of any sort are rare and often only recognized within limited domains. Moreover, as Glaser and Strauss asserted, in line with the Pragmatist roots of GTM, a grounded theory often proves to be of 'great practical use long before the theory is tested with great rigor' (1965b, p. 293). In response to such challenges, I offer Joseph Heller's retort when asked why none of his later books were as good as *Catch 22*.

Interviewer: 'Since *Catch 22*, you haven't written anything nearly as good.'
Heller: 'No, but then neither has anyone else.'

Momentous grounded theories, such as *Awareness*, *Time*, and *Status Passage* (Glaser & Strauss, 1965b, 1968, 1971), and 'supernormalizing' (Charmaz) are few and far between, but then so too are theories more generally. This is not a fault of GTM.

So where is the theory in grounded theory?

The challenging interrogatory is often used by those keen to point to and disparage poor examples of GTM, often amounting to no more than a series of re-descriptions of some aspects of a research context, presented in the form of 'codes' with little or no conceptualization. This specific issue has been dealt with already, but it is worth reiterating the point that it is not hard to find poor uses of any and every method, yet it would be wrong to fault a method itself based only on such examples. This specific challenge, however, begs the question of what is meant by the term 'theory', both for GTM as such and more generally.

The meaning of the term *theory* is itself fraught with ambiguity and ambivalence (Bryant, 2009).

> For some the term is an accolade, so citations for Nobel prizes mention that the winners have made major contributions to one or another theory, or have developed a new one. In contrast, anyone wishing to disparage something might use the term in precisely the opposite sense, hence those arguing in favour of Intelligent Design refer to the work of Charles Darwin or the concept of evolution in general as ***only*** *a theory*. (Bryant, 2017, p. 98)

'Theory' is best understood as a sensitizing concept in the early GTM writings, but since then the term has understandably been the focus of greater scrutiny and substantive analysis. Several chapters in *Current Developments* reflect this, offering a range of definitions and discussions on the topic.

Johnson and Walsh (CD:25) note that there are different ways of defining theory. These range from 'general, etic (nomothetic) or particular, local, emic (idiographic) perspectives'. The differences are largely derived from differing positions with regard to epistemology and ontology, so from a

> positivist or postpositivist view ... a theory could be 'a system of constructs and variables in which the constructs are related to each other by propositions and the variables are related to each other by hypotheses' (Bacharach, 1989, p. 498). [For constructivists/interpretivists a] theory could be an 'approximation' of a complex reality (Weick, 1995).

They refer to Gregor's definition, which

> proposed a broad, all-encompassing definition of a theory as an abstract entity that aims 'to describe, explain, and enhance understanding of the world and, in some cases, to provide predictions of what will happen in the future and to give a basis for intervention and action' (Gregor, 2006, p. 616).

Cathy Urquhart (CD:4) also uses Gregor's definition, noting that 'Gregor also defines the components of all theories as containing a means of representation, constructs, statements of relationship, and scope'. Birks and Mills (CD:12) define a theory as 'an explanatory scheme comprising a set of concepts related to each other through logical patterns of connectivity'.

Kelle (CD:3) takes a different approach, quoting

> a famous metaphor of Hempel, a theory is a network of terms (following our terminology we would say 'categories') which 'floats, as it were, above the plane of observation and is anchored to it by rules of interpretation'. These rules of interpretation link certain points of the network 'with specific places in the plane of observation...: From certain observational data, we may ascend, via an interpretive string, to some point in the theoretical network, thence proceed, via definitions and hypotheses to other points, from which another interpretive string permits a descent to the plane of observation' (Hempel, 1952, p. 36).

Kelle's chapter is devoted specifically to this subject, and he offers both a general overview of the term, as well as discussing how it relates to GTM, arguing that Glaser and Strauss's understanding of the nature of theories was centred on categories.

> ... the concept of 'category' played a crucial role: categories are not only the building blocks and basic elements of theories, they are also important tools used throughout the whole research process to develop full-fledged theories. Theoretical statements (or in other words, 'hypotheses') are basically formed by connecting categories.

The nature of a theory is then far from simple or obvious and needs to be addressed. In *Discovery*, Glaser and Strauss drew on Merton's (1949) work, in which he argued for 'theories of the middle range'.

> Theories that lie between the minor but necessary working hypotheses that evolve in abundance during day-to-day research and the all-inclusive systematic efforts to develop a unified theory that will explain all the observed uniformities of social behaviour, social organization and social change. (Merton, quoted by Glaser and Strauss, 1967, p. 39)

Merton argued that such theories were developed from close scrutiny of the data, and developed from studies of specific and constrained contexts. Glaser and Strauss adopted this approach in describing both *substantive* and *formal* grounded theories as theories of the middle range. Kelle (CD:3) argues that '[A]s the scope of a substantive theory is extended towards a formal one, category or construct names by necessity become simpler, and more abstract, because that construct has to apply to a large number of substantive cases'.

I am not suggesting that anyone using GTM has to engage at great length with these debates, but care is needed in the use of the term 'theory', which should be accompanied by some form of further explanation. Again, this is an issue that extends beyond GTM to reporting research findings in general, although it is more pertinent to GTM with its inherent claim to be a method that can lead to new theories.

This all demonstrates that claims by researchers to have developed new theoretical insights need to be made and treated with caution, whether or not they have used GTM. Yet, unlike many other methods, GTM clearly offers the basis for such claims, albeit with critical caveats relating to scope and applicability, for instance, the point that GTs are theories of the middle range. Here again, an aspect of GTM that has been criticized should be seen as clarifying and facilitating good research practice. Other methods say little or nothing about these issues.

The relative silence regarding Pragmatism in the context of GTM is critical here. The Pragmatist view, derived from Dewey, James and others, is that a theory is a tool – to be judged accordingly. Grounded theorists should base their claims on this, whether or not they use the term 'theory', 'model', 'framework', or any equivalent one. Classic GTs, such as *Awareness*, *Time*, and *Status Passage* (Glaser & Strauss, 1965b, 1968, 1971), and 'supernormalizing' (Charmaz) have earned their status as *useful* conceptualizations. They are exceptional in the extent of their take-up and influence on practice. Other GTs may have had more limited influence, but that is not to undermine their derivation and use within specific contexts. I have argued elsewhere that Darwin can be seen as a proto-grounded theorist, and hence the theory of evolution as a highly 'useful' grounded theory (Bryant, 2017, Chapter 20). Few theories – grounded or otherwise – are as conceptually powerful as this.

Duckles et al. (CD:31) build upon the Pragmatist view of theories, combining it with Action Research. They encourage researchers to examine carefully how theories are constructed and their relationships to the research process.

> If theory is, as proposed, 'a grand word for these everyday activities of knowing, understanding and sense-making', then how is it uncovered and used to inform methods and practice? They [Dick, Stringer and Huxham (2009)] propose that we honor the theories of the communities we work with, both to clarify and understand the issues guiding our action research, and to strengthen processes of inquiry.

The issue of what is meant by 'theory', both in general terms and for GTM specifically, is complex. Some chapters in *Current Developments* cover the topic in substantive fashion, others refer to the issue as the basis for discussion of other concerns. In this sense, the term is treated as 'definitive' in some chapters, and as a 'sensitizing' concept in others.

As a conclusion to this brief discussion of the term, the following quote from Albert Hirschman seems apposite. Hirschman was a noted, albeit maverick, economist and essayist, his most widely cited work being *Exit, Voice and Loyalty*. In a discussion on the impact of his work he noted that '[T]he success of a theory consists … in that suddenly everyone begins to reason according to *new categories*' (1990 [1970], emphasis added). Hirschman was not a grounded theorist, but this seems to be a wonderfully succinct statement of one key criterion for judging any claim to theoretical innovation, particularly a grounded theory.

5

INDIGENEITY

One aspect of doing research, now the subject of critical scrutiny, is the way in which the research process is inevitably implicated with issues of power, domination, exploitation, and hegemony, also with cultural and political complexities and ramifications.

The 2007 *Handbook* included a chapter by O'Neil Green et al. (2007) which argued for the incorporation of issues of race and ethnicity as part of the research process. Various chapters in *Current Developments* develop this recommendation, stressing that researchers need to take account of various 'sensitizing concepts' – e.g. feminism, culture, social injustice, indigeneity, domination, hegemony, and emancipation. Some might take exception to this in the context of GTM, arguing that it precludes or impedes the process of open-minded initiation of research. Thus, Hadley (CD:28) notes that there are grounds both for and against the incorporation of emancipatory concerns in GTM and research more generally. On the other hand, he also refers to

> Adorno's critique of the sociologist Paul Lazarsfeld … a mentor of Glaser, and arguably the progenitor of Glaser's primary philosophical and methodological beliefs. From a [critical] perspective, Adorno denounced Lazarsfeld's preference for simply describing 'life as it is' as nothing more than 'a bourgeois sociology reinforcing the domination inherent in society' (Gibson, 2007, p. 438). Similar criticisms were levelled against Symbolic Interactionism, an early methodological forerunner of Grounded Theory Methodology (Fine, 1993).

Hadley quotes Kincheloe and McLaren, who state that theoretical descriptions 'are not simply about the world but serve to construct it … language in the form of discourses serves as a form of regulation and domination'

(2000, p. 284). From a constructivist/interpretivist position it is not possible to claim that data 'simply speaks for itself'.

Yet Glaser and Strauss were right to maintain that concepts – even sensitizing ones – have 'to earn their way'. This is not required each and every time a concept is used as a resource in someone's research. In *Discovery*, the concepts of 'data' and 'theory' are not the subject of clear and definitive discussion, in Blumer's terms they 'lack precise reference and have no bench marks which allow a clean-cut identification of a specific instance and of its content. Instead, they rest on a general sense of what is relevant' (1954, p. 7). Similarly, Hesse-Biber and Flowers (CD:24) state that 'feminism supplies the perspective and the disciplines supply the method. The feminist researcher exists at their intersection'. Irwin (CD:18) discusses GTM research undertaken in 'the context of masculinity and violence', and Ravi Priya (CD:19) echoes this with regards to research on 'suffering and healing'. Other GTM researchers develop their work from positions explicitly developed around topics such as ethnicity, social deprivation, and other forms of inequality (see below).

Again, GTM can be a source for better research practice in general if this leads to the expectation for all research reports to incorporate a brief introductory section where researchers clarify any sensitizing concepts that informed their work, albeit that such considerations could at best be indicative rather than definitive, since others might readily point out other aspects that were unacknowledged or tacitly assumed.

Morse and Clark (CD:7) deal with some of the ramifications of all this in their chapter on sampling, explaining that seeking to deal with ethnicity, for instance, 'is tricky. You must determine if your sample should be cohesive culturally/ethnically'. Again, there is no once-and-for-all solution, but researchers must ensure that, as far as possible, they clearly state and justify their orientation and any other related issues/concepts that they decide to incorporate within their research approach.

Charmaz has specifically developed GTM as a basis for research in areas that touch upon and are even constituted by concerns for social justice (see below). Kathy and I were particularly concerned to invite contributions to *Current Developments* from a wide range of contributors, particularly from geo-political and linguistic groups not included in the earlier volume, although there is still a predominance of Anglophone and German-speaking contributors. We were keen for contributors to take account of the ways in which research is conducted on a global and international scale – including collaborations between researchers from different backgrounds, countries, continents, and regions – and also with doctoral students undertaking their research and gaining doctoral guidance in universities in foreign countries.

One of the terms that many authors use is indigeneity. Norm Denzin (CD:22) centres his discussion around this, making the case and space for communities to determine what is and is not acceptable research as it 'encourages self-determination and empowerment'. He coins the term 'indigenous grounded theory inquiry', arguing that it

> connects research to struggles for liberation, to struggles which empower, which challenge the status quo, rebuild leadership, restore environments, and revitalize language, culture, and community (Smith, 2005: 89). 'Indigenous grounded theory research is performative research carried out by indigenous scholars, in and for indigenous communities, using the principles of indigenous grounded theory inquiry' (Smith, 2005: 89). This form of inquiry is collaborative and participatory and is characterized by the absence of a need to be in control, by a desire to be connected to and to be a part of a moral community where a primary goal is the compassionate understanding of another's moral position (Bishop, 1998: 203).

Norm Denzin has been a towering force for good in the world of methods for many years. He worked with Lindesmith and Strauss from the 1970s, co-editing several editions of their key text on social psychology. His early work *The Research Act* (1970) was hailed by many, including Herbert Blumer, as a revolutionary text on the topic. Starting in the 1980s, he has co-edited an enormous number of key collections on research methods, as well as organizing international conferences and summer schools. Denzin has co-edited the *Handbook of Qualitative Research*, through its many editions (Denzin & Lincoln, 1994, 2000, 2001, 2005, 2017), and also a range of other collections, including *Qualitative Inquiry and Human Rights* (2010), *Qualitative Inquiry and Social Justice* (2009), *Handbook of Critical Indigenous Inquiry* (2008), and *Performance Ethnography: The Politics and Pedagogies of Culture* (2003).

It is therefore with some trepidation that I take issue with aspects of his chapter. I concur with Denzin's sentiments, but believe that the way in which he expresses them needs further examination if they are 'to earn their way'. He uses the terms 'performance' and 'performative' almost as synonyms, which is misleading. In so doing, he also fails to give proper attention to the latter, which is a critical issue in the context of his argument and the ways in which research needs to develop a genuinely cosmopolitan orientation. It may well be that his extended discussions in *Performance Ethnography* resolve this, but the term 'performativity' resonates across many disciplines and now has attained a highly specific range of meanings and ramifications.

In the extract in the earlier paragraph, he attributes the phrase 'performative research' to Linda Tuhiwai Smith, although it does not actually appear in the work cited. It may be that the term, in Denzin's and Smith's contexts, is a derivation from the concept of 'performance', but it then needs to be distinguished from the far more widely understood use of 'performative'.

The most notable and influential use of the word 'performative' is in the writings of the philosopher J. L. Austin, particularly *How to Do Things with Words* (1962). His work was taken up by John Searle in *Speech Acts* (1969), and more recently by Judith Butler in the context of gender. Butler specifically distinguishes between performance and performativity as follows:

> *It's one thing to say that gender is performed and that is a little different from saying gender is performative.* When we say gender is performed we usually mean that we've taken on a role or we're acting in some way and that our acting or our role-playing is crucial to the gender that we are and the gender that we present to the world. To say that gender is performative is a little different *because for something to be performative means that it produces a series of effects.* We act and walk and speak and talk in ways that consolidate an impression of being a man or being a woman. (Butler, 2013, emphasis added)

If applied to the context of 'doing research' this is an important distinction. Research as an activity cannot be seen as a dispassionate and neutral form of investigation, but as constitutive and formative; it simultaneously incorporates some features and marginalizes, excludes, or evades others. Strauss's work on identity, particularly *Mirrors and Masks* (1959), alludes precisely to these ideas, albeit expressed in a different vocabulary. To some extent they were also present in early GTM, but it is only in recent work, such as that by Charmaz, that they have begun to be clearly articulated.

Once research is seen as performative, however, it must be understood that, as Butler argues, all research 'produces a series of effects'. These effects are largely beyond the control of researchers. Hence, Butler's point that 'performativity' has ramifications and dimensions that extend well beyond 'role-play'. Moreover, the concept of performativity applies to all forms of research, including indigenous research – i.e. there will be ramifications for these forms of research, as there are for all other forms, albeit very distinct from and all-too-often over-powered and effaced by 'Western' ones. This is almost certainly what Denzin means in his chapter, but the point needs to be put across more clearly and with due regard to the ways in which the terms 'performance' and 'performativity' are now construed.

Denzin presents the ideas of Smith, derived from *Decolonizing Methodologies: Research and Indigenous Peoples* (Smith, 2012), which are encapsulated in the phrase from the introduction: '"Research" is probably one of the dirtiest words in the indigenous world's vocabulary'. She counters the predominant Western assumptions on the nature of research and knowledge from the position of an indigenous and colonized Māori woman, calling for the decolonization of methodologies and a new agenda for indigenous research, one concerned with 'a more critical understanding of the underlying assumptions, motivations and values that inform research practices'. I fully concur with this, but the concept of 'indigenous research' must itself be examined to see how it 'earns its way'.

Denzin (CD:22) treats the concept of 'indigeneity', and associated terms such as 'ritual' and 'culture', as given:

> The performance of sacred tribal rituals, the telling of oral histories, and the performance of sacred identities validates traditional ways of life. The performances embody the ritual. They are the ritual. In this sense the performance becomes a form of public pedagogy. It uses a performative aesthetic to foreground cultural meaning, and to teach these meanings to performers and audience members alike.

This is fine, but it must also be understood that in most, probably all, cultures the performance of rituals and rites is bound up with hierarchies of power and inequalities, particularly gender-based ones. They also incorporate forms of taboo, phobias, and prejudices; usually in the form of differentiating between us/insider and them/outsider, with the latter split between the 'acceptable' or tolerable, and the undesirable.

Smith points out the ways in which many assumptions around research practice in 'the West' are bound up with discriminatory and biased views and ramifications; all in need of exposure and remedy. But the practices of 'others' need similar scrutiny, even though they are far less influential and globally damaging in their current forms.

Denzin develops and extends Smith's argument, but he risks undermining its force and significance. For instance, in discussing the importance of research giving voice to all participants, he wants researchers to 'resist speaking for the other'; but this is an impossibility. Even researchers from within an indigenous culture cannot avoid 'speaking for others'; we must not fall prey to the mistake of treating 'other cultures', or indeed our 'own' culture, as homogeneous. After all, in one way or another any researcher writing anything with a view to publication is speaking for others. (It might be thought that using auto-ethnography partially resolves this, but such auto-biographical approaches can often become part of the problem rather than a possible solution.)

Focusing on indigeneity should be part of a process of critical scrutiny of issues around power relationships, dominance, hegemony, class, colonialism, and post-colonialism. It should also be part of the reflexivity that is an essential consideration for all researchers. As a rule of thumb, when encountering terms such as 'we', 'our', or any equivalent terms, it is almost always crucial to ask who is included and/or excluded, and what is assumed in such generalizations.[1]

Denzin (CD:22) correctly stresses that '[I]ndigenous knowledge systems are too frequently turned into objects of study, treated as if they were instances of quaint folk theory held by the members of a primitive culture'. The corollary of this is that the decolonizing project 'reverses this equation, making Western systems of knowledge the object of inquiry'. Denzin wonders whether or not this is the basis for 'a dialogue between different systems/ discourses'. It certainly should be, but not if this leads to sacralizing and sentimentalizing 'other cultures' and 'indigeneity'. Denzin (CD:22) states that:

> [T]heory, method, and epistemology are aligned in this project, anchored in the moral philosophies that are taken for granted in indigenous cultures and language communities. A pedagogy of emancipation and empowerment is endorsed, a pedagogy that encourages struggles for autonomy, cultural well-being, cooperation, and collective.

But, unfortunately, this cannot be taken at face value. Emancipation and empowerment, together with autonomy and cooperation, are powerful sensitizing concepts, but they have to earn their way, and be amenable to critical scrutiny.

Denzin treats GTM as a touchstone, embodying the standard for relatively good practice, but to be contrasted with some new form of 'better practice'. In so doing, he sets up GTM versus ethnography:

Grounded theory is a performance, a set of performative and interpretive practices and ways of making the world visible. This commitment to visibility is
anchored in the belief that the world, at some level, is orderly, and patterned.
The world of social interaction and social experience can be theoretically sam-
pled, saturated, located in situational social world, arena mapped, coded, fitted
into conceptual categories, diagrammed, placed in conditional and consequen-
tial matrices, and represented in narrative, visual, and historical discourses. These
discourses, in turn, can be analyzed in terms of social relationships, identities, and
intersecting arenas and social worlds. (Denzin, CD:22)

This is then contrasted with ethnography:

In contrast, the performance ethnographer is a troublemaker. The practices of
ethnography are not tools for creating order out of chaos. Instead ethnographies
are for creating chaos, ways of disrupting the world and its representations.
Performance ethnographers see disorder in the world, reading orderliness as a
dramaturgical production. (Denzin, CD:22)

This may be a reasonable characterization of some forms of current ethnography, albeit that ethnography, as originally developed in the 18th and
19th centuries, was intimately associated with conquest, colonialism, and
'scientific' models of racial hierarchies – i.e. what Smith had in mind when
referring to 'research' as one of the 'dirtiest words in the indigenous world's
vocabulary'.

It should also be noted that Glaser and Strauss specifically criticized ethnography as one form of research that was incapable of generating theory.

Denzin is also off-target with his other criticisms since GTM writers have
always stressed that grounded theories are modifiable and embrace contingency, uncertainty, and ambivalence. This is particularly the case for those
who argue that GTM encompasses constructivist and Pragmatist ideas concerning the provisional and contingent nature of knowledge claims and
conceptual constructs. Grounded theorists have in many instances proved
themselves to be effective troublemakers.

I referred earlier to Burawoy's criticism that, in letting data speak for itself,
grounded theorists were leaving the world as it is, tacitly supporting the
status quo. But this is to mistake the potential impact of theoretical descriptions in general, and particularly those emanating from the social actors
themselves. Recent GTM work has focused on issues around social justice and
inequality, giving voice to those challenging conventional and hegemonic

discourses. Charmaz leads the way, arguing that GTM, through its lineage with Symbolic Interaction and Pragmatism, inherently encompasses issues of social justice and critical inquiry, a theme that Duckles et al. (CD:31) develop. I am sure Denzin would concur with all of this, so it is unfortunate that he sees the need to make the distinction between GTM and performance ethnography.

Denzin (CD:22) offers a set of questions for the meta-level of research derived from a 'critical politics of interpretation'. He argues that these should be posed by indigenous scholars with regards to 'any research project, including those projects guided by grounded critical theory'. The questions, however, will be familiar to anyone applying for a research grant from any government or private funding body. Questions regarding ownership, priority, personnel, and likely beneficiaries are all now part of the standard Western research funding process.

A non-Westernized orientation certainly leads to a different understanding of 'we' in Denzin's questions, such as 'What research do *we* want done?' and 'How will *we* know it is worthwhile?' But Denzin goes further than this, stating that 'These questions are addressed to indigenous and non-indigenous scholars alike. They must be answered in the affirmative; that is, indigenists must conduct, own, and benefit from any research that is done on or for them.' Unfortunately, several of the questions cannot be answered either affirmatively or negatively – e.g. the two at the start of this paragraph. More critically, however, this approach risks compartmentalizing research and researchers into indigenists and non-indigenists, again committing the error of false attribution of homogeneity; effectively implying that non-indigenists cannot participate in the research contexts of the former. This is not the basis for the type of dialogue that ought to be one vital outcome from more highly developed research awareness contexts, which is surely what Denzin is keen to encourage.

Duckles et al. (CD:31) provide a useful corrective in their discussion:

Community-based participatory research (CBPR) provides an orientation to research that *'emphasizes issues of trust, power, dialogue, community capacity building, and collaborative inquiry toward the goal of social change'* (Minkler & Wallerstein, 2011, p. 7). Core characteristics of this approach include its focus on *co-learning and the balance between research and action* (Israel et al., 2005) as well as *creating local knowledge and promoting systems change* (Minkler & Wallerstein, 2011). (emphasis added)

Duckles et al. use the term 'community', itself the topic of extensive critical discussion – e.g. Bauman's (1971) *Community: Seeking Safety in an Insecure World*. But in so doing they make several important points with regards to researchers, their methodological assumptions, and the role of all of those involved in research practices.

> As researchers, we are aware that, at times, *we can be drawn toward a tacit methodological and theoretical individualism*. This threat partially emerges from the university paradigms of research and publishing that often privilege certain notions of expertise and singular voices. In addition, we recognize the individualism that underlies many Anglo-American cultures. Instead, *we work toward explicitly integrating multiple methodologies, adopting diverse theoretical traditions to guide our work and embracing abductive reasoning to reach into local ways of understanding*. Our goal, however, is not to adopt this integration as another singular process, or to find and bring exclusive sensitizing concepts to our analysis. Instead, we heed Lincoln and Guba's (2013) *caution against developing an 'epistemological or theoretical melting pot* in which researchers come to share lenses or standpoints (which have primarily been Eurocentric) and instead, *to adopt approaches that bring attention and understanding to the nuances of difference*' (p. 10). (emphasis added)

It is important for researchers to understand that the 'nuances of difference' are common across these approaches, albeit that to date they have mostly operated forcefully in only one direction. Crossman and Noma (CD:29) take some account of this in their chapter on 'internationalization', although in using the concept of a paradigm in referring to 'a researcher's epistemological and ontological premises', they introduce the problem of incommensurability that was referred to earlier, even if they do invoke Denzin and Lincoln's concept of 'multiple paradigms interacting in dynamic ways with one another'.

Directly countering Denzin, Bainbridge et al. (CD:30) stress that it is precisely the grounded theory approach that can 'work to ameliorate some of the critiques that Indigenous people have about conventional research processes and their continuing failure to deliver benefits'. Their chapter describes six key critiques that 'Indigenous nations have made of conventional research approaches'.

> (1) narrowly-focused, reductionist thinking; (2) a preponderance of deficit-focused descriptive research that is of generally suboptimal methodological quality; (3) issues of power and control; (4) devaluing of Indigenous knowledge systems; (5) onerous amounts of research without corresponding impact; and (6) context-independent and culturally-insensitive research.

Seeking to respond to these critiques offers a useful starting point for consideration of issues around indigeneity and post-colonial dialogue across differing perspectives and positions regarding the status of knowledge and truth claims. Bainbridge et al. 'specifically account for how the seemingly disparate methodologies of phronetic social sciences and participatory action research approaches can be integrated with constructivist grounded theory methods to make issues of social justice explicit in the research endeavour'. (*Phronetic in this context is derived from* the classical Greek concept *phronesis*, which can be understood to mean practical judgement or practical wisdom.)

Echoing some of my foregoing critique of Denzin, they argue that:

> The very issues that many researchers and others are attempting to resolve *for* Indigenous people are the products of imposing Western systems and knowledge. Paradoxically, proposed solutions often derive from and are implemented through the same power dynamics and reductionist thinking that precipitated the concerns in the first instance. These impositions both reinforce Western authority as *the* knowers, disparage Indigenous knowledges, embed ethnocentric assumptions and practices and enact parochial solutions that further entrench social problems and impede cultural survival and flourishing. (Bainbridge et al., CD:30, emphasis in the original)

I concur with this, with the caveat that ethnocentrism is a failing and a fallacy common across cultures and ethnicities, although emphatically not in equal measures or degree, nor in ramifications and consequences. Efforts to dismantle and neutralize ethnocentrism must begin with and be focused explicitly upon the most destructive and disparaging forms emanating from 'imposing Western systems'.

Current Developments encompasses several discussions of 'culture'. Crossman and Noma (CD:29) note Charmaz's influence in setting the agenda. 'Charmaz (2014b) has argued that the cultural, economic, historical, political and geographic conditions of the United States have determined the logic, values, epistemological assumptions and worldview that influence the kinds of problems investigated and the research questions posed within grounded theory'. They point out the irony in Charmaz's (2014b) view that, 'despite the widespread exportation of grounded theory to study phenomena in a variety of cultures, few scholars have explored the cultural assumptions that underpin the methodology itself'.

Yet researchers need to avoid assumptions that cultures are hermetic, distinct, and homogeneous. Clarke (CD:1) offers a succinct corrective in her characterization of the interpretative turn, asserting that 'Cultures are best understood as unevenly changing assemblages of distinctive symbols and signifying practices'.

Reichertz (CD:13) enhances this arguing that:

> The social order around which humans (often but not always) orient themselves in their actions is constantly changing and is, moreover, 'sub-culturally fragmented' in the sense, that each sub-culture develops its own symbolic and social order. The different order(s) therefore possess only a localized validity and are continually and, since the advent of the 'modern', with increasing rapidity being changed by individuals who previously (up to a point) adhered to them (Eisenstadt, 2003; Foucault, 2004).

Crossman and Noma (CD:29) explain that 'little is known about the implications of globalization and, more specifically, internationalization, for the teaching, learning, practice and development of grounded theory'. This leads to the issue of doing research in a non-English context, with the expectation that the final output will be written in English. Massimiliano Tarozzi (CD:9) discusses this in the context of translation, starting from the position that 'the researcher is a culturally defined subject and analysis is embedded in processes of mutual meaning-making'. He looks at the complexities of translation in research, not simply confined to GTM. This concerns

> (1) using GTM in cultures and countries in which researchers would be using the translation, (2) issues arising when international researchers are using the original GTM sources in English but conducting their studies in their native languages, and (3) presenting research results in English of data collected and analyzed in other languages. (Tarozzi, CD:9)

Many of my doctoral students have used GTM, and most of these have been non-UK students, many based in countries outside Europe and the USA. They have undertaken interviews and other forms of data collection in their local language(s), then developed their GTs in English. In most cases they translated their data into English, coding from that translation. Recently, however, one or two have compared the outcomes of this route with an alternative: completing the initial coding in the original language, then translating the codes into English. Although the sample is too small to draw any conclusions regarding any differences in the outcomes, students who tried both routes reported no significant differences in the results. When using both routes, they did, however, note significant enhancements in their understanding of the complexities of coding, and developed a clearer grasp of the process for articulating higher-level abstractions and concepts. To this extent, having to gather, code, and analyze data across two or more languages offered a distinct advantage, albeit only after significant additional effort.

Taking indigeneity, cultural and ethnic difference, translation, ethnocentricity, power, and dominance into account complicates consideration of what is involved in coding, and researchers need to develop an understanding of their research actions that takes account of some, if not all, of these. Hadley (CD:28) refers to Clarke's work on *Situational Analysis* and the influence of postmodernism in concluding that 'definitions about what is real are in a constant state of flux, and the methodology will reflect this chaos. Coding is deconstructive and similar to postmodern art, in that it is constantly being transformed and reinterpreted by each individual.' This is Hadley's conclusion, not Clarke's, and potentially opens the way for the 'methodological and theoretical individualism' Duckles et al. (CD:31) warn against. As was pointed out above, research results, even interim ones that result from early stages of coding, need some claims to consistency, coherence, credibility, and rigour. I have already used Rorty's provocative contention that 'Truth is what your contemporaries allow you to get away with' (See Chapter 3, p. 80, note 5). A somewhat bizarre and challenging claim, but one that does clearly involve gaining the assent of others, not simply deciding things for oneself.

Note

1   A joke dating from the 1960s provides an insightful, if ironic, example. The Lone Ranger and Tonto are watching a horde of Indian braves bear down on them in full battle fury. 'Looks like we're in trouble, Tonto,' says the Lone Ranger to his pal. 'What do you mean "we," white man?' Tonto responds... (It is now attributed to E. Nelson Bridwell when writing gags for *MAD Magazine*.) http://pancocojams. blogspot.co.uk/2013/07/sources-meanings-of-what-do-you-mean.html. For any reader perplexed by this reference to *The Lone Ranger*, I recommend Wikipedia and YouTube.

6

STUDENT AND LEARNING ISSUES

I have remarked upon the paradox that some writers on GTM argue that using the method is easy and comes naturally, simultaneously arguing that conceptualizing is difficult and something that some may not be able to accomplish. Glaser exemplifies this, probably a result of his aim to offer guidance and establish confidence in novice users of GTM, and also to caution against the idea that 'anything goes' when developing concepts grounded in the data. It would, however, be better to acknowledge that conceptualization is a skill that requires practice and experience, including learning from one's own – and others' – mistakes. In other words, researchers need to develop precisely the *theoretical sensitivity* that was key to GTM from the start. This form of guidance comes more naturally with a constructivist view of GTM than from one that implies or openly states that the concepts/theories somehow emerge from the data.

Another issue emanates from the protracted discussions regarding the status of differing variants of GTM, which complicate the process of anyone keen to learn about GTM. This is in part what Crossman and Noma (CD:29) refer to as the 'tricky spaces' that students need to navigate in their research. Morse and Clark (CD:7) argue that sampling while trying to account for ethnicity is 'tricky', and Denzin makes extensive use of Smith's critique of 'colonialist methods', including her chapter 'On Tricky Ground' (Smith, 2005).

This is not a promising basis for novice researchers who are keen to gain confidence and develop novel insights and concepts. So, students can be forgiven if they discount GTM as a forbidding and obstacle-strewn option rather than as a confidence-boosting one. This is not unique to GTM; it is another form of criticism that applies generally. Texts on methods are never able fully to explain the intricacies in using them in actual projects, just as reading books on mountaineering or playing the cello are not going to lead in themselves to conquering Everest or performing at Carnegie Hall.

In similar vein, Irwin (CD:18) explains how she felt herself to be a 'GTM pretender', something she overcame once she encountered Charmaz's constructivist approach, which helped her realize 'that others were probably grappling with the same constraints within the various GTM statements that troubled me'. Irwin was sceptical regarding 'the effort to discover a unitary, basic social process encompassing all individuals' experiences in a setting'. She was frustrated in her attempts to use Strauss and Corbin's conditional matrix (Strauss and Corbin, 1990 & 1998), and so was reassured that 'Charmaz's (2006, p. xi) "flexible approach" invited skeptical researchers like me to "enter the methodological fray" and "messy" debates about methods'.

Crossman and Noma (CD:29) argue that discussion of GTM-in-use by graduate students is an underdeveloped area in grounded theory publications. There is, however, a growing literature on GTM-in-use; some accounts are available through *The Grounded Theory Institute*, and my recent book includes four verbatim accounts from doctoral students (Bryant, 2017, Chapter 19). Reading these should be useful for research students and others, although there is no substitute for actual experience, learning from one's mistakes, successes, and insights. Undertaking a research project and learning about different methods are basic requirements for developing and honing one's *methodological sensitivity*.

I have referred to the uniquely hostile attitude of many academics and other gate-keepers with regards to GTM. One consequence is that many students are discouraged from learning more about the method and its possible use in their research. Paradoxically, given the popularity and renown of GTM, many academics, with a barely minimal understanding of the method, offer to advise students in their GTM-based research. Stern's concept of 'minus mentoring' was discussed earlier. It refers to well-meaning advisors with at best only a cursory understanding of the method. Stern was an adherent of Glaser's variant of GTM, and her criticism was aimed not only at those professing to know more about GTM than was actually the case, but also at those who may well have known a good deal about the method, but who, in Stern's view, had taken a different path from Glaser – particularly Strauss's later work and his collaboration with Corbin.

Those with experience of GTM must ensure that researchers relying on them for guidance are fully appraised about the method and its variants and nuances. On the other hand, any *over-mentoring* must also be avoided. Mentoring GTM research requires a balance between offering guidance and refraining from prompting or influencing the student's progress from coding to analysis. Students should be encouraged to articulate their findings at various stages of their research, and, if possible, to discuss these with their peers, even if the latter are not using GTM. Opportunities to do so, however, are dependent on there being a suitably large and willing community of researchers, either readily at hand or through workshops or seminars organized on a wider basis.

Once students have developed some of their analysis, guidance can be offered relating to possible ways forward, including directing them to the appropriate literature and other sources with which they should engage. Most commonly, this occurs once a more developed form of model or theory has been established, but it can also take place earlier, as initial coding or secondary coding results in a semi-stable set of codes, categories, and/or concepts.

Mentors may, however, differ with regard to the extent to which they persuade or influence students to articulate and refine their analyses as social processes incorporating gerunds. (The Wikipedia entry on gerunds in various languages is a useful starting point to learn more – see https://en.wikipedia.org/wiki/Gerund#Gerunds_in_various_languages; see also Bryant, 2017, Introduction to Part Three.)

As was explained earlier, the relationship between GTM and sociology is paradoxical, but GTM is best seen as a method that facilitates the development of insights into and encapsulations of social processes; hence the importance of gerunds, which combine aspects of both a noun and a verb. Yet students should not feel obliged to develop their concepts/categories as gerunds from the outset, and in many cases they may find that they lack the relevant expertise in sociological thinking to conceptualize a social process. Some direction may well be appropriate and necessary at this stage, although the ability to 'think sociologically' (see above, and Bauman & May, 2001) requires skill and practice, including trial-and-error and subsequent reflection leading to enhanced *methodological and theoretical sensitivity*.

If students and their mentors can find the balance between minus mentoring and over-mentoring, there may still be problems in dealing with academic gate-keepers – whether in the form of examiners, review boards, or evaluators. People in these positions cannot be expected to be fully cognizant with every research method, tool, and technique; but if they are confronted with something that is out of their comfort zone, their assumption ought to be that they should refrain from pre-emptive and ill-informed judgements, and defer to and seek assistance from those with relevant expertise. This is common practice when, for instance, a research proposal incorporates complex and sophisticated statistical techniques and digital tools. An evaluator with little or no experience with quantitative research will understand that assessment in such cases is best left to others. Unfortunately, the converse seems not to apply; those with little or no experience of qualitative research rarely excuse themselves in the same manner. Furthermore, GTM is often singled out for criticism, based on the sort of misplaced and ill-informed preconceptions and prejudices referred to earlier as 'a strange hostility'. It is one thing to criticize a research proposal for the ways in which a method or technique is planned to be used, or a research report – such as a PhD thesis – in which its use is explained, but quite another to censure or deplore a method or technique itself. I have sought to offer guidance to students, mentors, and gate-keepers on these issues (Bryant, 2017, Chapter 18).

Presentation of GTM research

My extensive experience with supervising, mentoring, and examining PhD students has demonstrated the different ways in which researchers present their findings, often enhancing textual descriptions with visualizations. Sometimes these derive directly from one or other form of CAQDAS, but many develop their own forms of presentation, sometimes to supplement CAQDAS outputs, but mostly as ways of enhancing the cogency of their presentation. Students often request examples of previous work using GTM, for example, doctoral dissertations or journal articles, as guides for their own work. But these can be more distracting than beneficial, and it is far better to work out one's own best form of presentation, albeit guided by any institutional conventions. Gorra (CD:15) argues that the current generation of students largely expect to use some form of digital technology in their research, including one or more forms of visualization. These must never be allowed simply to stand on their own; all require textual explanation and justification. Konecki's (CD:17) concept of 'multi-slice imaginings' applies to all forms of visualization, including those used in doctoral dissertations and other research reports. So it is incumbent on researchers to explain and contextualize any visualizations included in their presentations.

The presentation of GTM research has changed over the years. *Awareness* and *Time* were published as research monographs (Glaser & Strauss, 1965b, 1968), as extended textual accounts of the research context and findings. In recent years a wide variety of formats and layouts have been used in research journals, PhD theses, and other extended accounts. In most cases, authors include details of the codes and the data from which they were derived, often using diagrams or other visualizations highlighting the processes involved in moving from data to codes. Other visualizations are then employed for later levels of analysis, sometimes leading to intricate and sophisticated representations of the eventual grounded theory.

Memos are also often incorporated into accounts in the form of verbatim extracts in clearly demarcated text boxes. If authors use this strategy, they must also ensure that they provide clear explanations and justification for the substantive topics indicated in the memos; unadorned memos cannot simply stand alone.

Both Glaser and Charmaz refer to 'theoretical sorting', in which memos are 'sorted' and clustered as a key component of preparation for drafting the research account. In *Constructing Grounded Theory*, Charmaz groups theoretical sorting, diagramming, and integrating as intertwined processes that researchers should undertake 'in the service of theoretical development of their analysis' (2006, p. 115).

Writers on GTM offer a variety of ways in which research can be presented, but individual researchers need to develop their own ways of ensuring that their presentations have effective impact on their target readership(s). Again, this is something that researchers need to develop through practice and experimentation, taking account of any specific regulations or institutional guidelines that may apply, but balancing this with consideration of the most effective forms of presentation – indicating how the research was carried out as well as presenting the findings and conclusions.

GTM and the literature

One aspect that continues to prove troublesome for students and others is how to relate to the literature when using GTM. The early admonition not to read the literature is best regarded as an historical accident, which was understandable in the context of social science in the USA in 1960s, but never really defensible for researchers keen to understand how their project might result in a 'contribution to knowledge'. Unfortunately, this canard has taken on an extended life of its own, and is resistant to efforts aimed at its eradication. It continues to mislead and deceive prospective GTM researchers, advisors, and others. The chapters by Martin (CD:11), and Thornberg and Dunne (CD:10) offer important clarifications of the ways in which literature can and should be used in GTM. These build upon previous accounts, such as Covan's (2007) chapter in the 2007 *Handbook*.

Thornberg and Dunne (CD:10) make a strong case for GTM researchers gaining familiarity with the relevant literature from the start, arguing that GTM research is 'necessary [when] the literature does not provide enough theories to cover all aspects or areas of the social life'. Moreover, even if existing theories seem immune from this deficiency, 'extant theories seldom fit or work, nor are relevant or sufficiently understandable to use in research which aspires to be sensitive to the empirical field and its participants'. This is a useful way of couching the argument, since it replaces a proscription with a constructive instruction and positive recommendation. While noting that Charmaz has described the original admonition as 'rhetorical', Thornberg and Dunne's chapter describes 'the place of the literature review in [the Glaserian, Straussian, constructivist] major versions of GTM'. Their general point is that engaging with the literature can be accomplished so that researchers relate their work to and integrate it with existing theories, but without undermining the data or forcing the analysis.

They distinguish between different forms and phases of using the literature: initial, ongoing, and final. The initial phase is discussed as part of the scoping exercise that provides the basis for further work. Rather than a constraint or contamination, this initial literature review should be 'both empowering and enriching, imbuing the researcher with the confidence to move forward with the study'.

The second phase is driven by the data and initial analysis: 'During this phase the researcher may seek to identify empirical studies which relate to findings (e.g., themes, ideas, hypotheses) emerging from the iterative process between data collection and analysis.' In many cases, this later exercise will incorporate literature that was not envisaged as relevant at the outset of the study.

The last phase is where

> the researcher seeks to contextualize the constructed grounded theory in rela-
> tion to established theoretical ideas and identify theoretical reference points
> against which to compare and contrast the data. This review is crucial in terms
> of locating the study within or across disciplines. Indeed, some of the theories
> which strongly resonate with a constructed grounded theory may be new to a
> given field or discipline. (Thornberg & Dunne, CD:10)

Thornberg and Dunne specifically relate use of literature to abduction, which they understand as 'a selective and creative process in which the researcher carefully examines which hypothesis explains a particular case or segment of data better than any other candidate hypotheses for further investigation'. They conclude that literature is 'a vital resource when conducting abduction in GTM'.

Martin (CD:11) offers a further and important perspective: using literature as data, specifically in the development of a formal grounded theory. She makes the case for 'four phases' in which the literature is addressed – 'scoping the literature, sampling the literature, bridging the literature, and confirming the theory' – relating each to 'the various stages of grounded theory methodology'.

Don't call it 'a literature review'!

Thornberg and Dunne (CD:10), and many others, refer to the 'literature review' in their discussions, even though they encompass far more than the usual meaning of the term – i.e. an initial phase of research aimed at positioning the research objectives from the start. My view is that doctoral students in particular are best advised to restrict the term to this initial stage, referring to later stages as part of their *theoretical coding* and/or as a 'return to' or 'engagement with' the literature. This will then preclude an all-too-common issue whereby well-meaning examiners ask: 'Why are there two literature review chapters in your thesis, an early chapter and a later one linked to the findings and conclusions?'

Martin (CD:11) and Thornberg and Dunne (CD:10) offer differing accounts of the ways in which the literature can and should be incorporated with GTM, and there are other authoritative sources that engage with this issue, for instance, Charmaz (2014a, Chapter 11) and Bryant (2017, Chapter 12). Students should familiarize themselves with these authoritative sources and clarify their own position, referring to one or more in their writing, thus anticipating any such queries and criticisms of this type. Taken together, this should provide the basis for dispelling the 'don't read the literature' canard, although it may still take some time before it finally disappears.

A repertoire of GTM research questions

Given that one of the key characteristics of GTM is that it eschews articulation of distinct and definitive research questions at the outset of any research project, it might seem strange that many GTM writers suggest a repertoire of initial research questions. In so doing, they acknowledge adding to and in some ways going beyond the generic questions that Glaser and Strauss offered as prompts to encourage and evoke wide-ranging responses at the initiation stage of a GTM-oriented project:

- What is this data about?
- What is this data a study of?
- What is going on?
- What are people doing?
- What are people saying?
- What do these actions and statements take for granted?[1]

Charmaz added to this list to include questions sensitizing researchers to different participants' viewpoints, issues of power and control, structure, and context, and the ways in which changes come about in the setting under investigation:

- From whose point of view is a given process fundamental?
- From whose is it marginal?
- How do the observed social processes emerge?
- How do participants' actions construct them?
- Who exerts control over these processes? Under what conditions?
- What meanings do different participants attribute to the process? How do they talk about it? What do they emphasize? What do they leave out?
- How and when do their meanings and actions concerning the process change? (Charmaz, 2006, p. 20)

Hesse-Biber and Flowers (CD:24) offer 'sensitizing questions' in their discussion of a 'Feminist Grounded Theory Approach':

- What particular research problems lend themselves to a feminist approach to mixed methods?
- How does a feminist approach to mixed methods research begin to take on a new context of research praxis?
- More specifically, how do feminist researchers tend to issues of power, authority, reflexivity, ethics, and difference in their mixed methods research design?
- How do and what are the reasons why feminist researchers deploy mixed methods research designs that utilize a grounded theory analysis?

Priya (CD:19) poses further questions, derived from his GTM-oriented research centred on suffering and healing:

- How does [the] paradigm shift in grounded theory methodology towards a Constructivist GT approach open up inquiry into various aspects of human and social world?
- What does it mean to be reflexive while collecting data and analyzing the same?
- Do empathy and compassion play a role in the process of data collection and analysis?
- Can the same data be viewed again from a different vantage point that might help further our insights into the studied phenomenon?

Hadley (CD:28) builds on both Glaser and Strauss's, and Charmaz's sets of questions, arguing that the former centre on 'what' and 'how' questions, the latter add 'why' as well as what and how questions, which can be framed as 'Why is this going on here?' He stresses that finding the answers will require further investigation into the background issues, contexts, and causes.

If there is an indication of recurring problems and social interactions intimately linked to power, inequality, gender, class stratification, or related critical concerns, further questions are then used to guide later memo-writing and coding:

- How is dominance being maintained here?
- What strategy is being used to privilege one group's narrative over another?
- How are things of value being gained here?
- How are things of value being lost here?

- What tactic is being used to gain an advantage over others here?
- What are the marginalizing interactions here?
- In what way is the disadvantaged resisting?
- How is gender/age/class affecting the dynamics discussed here?
- Who has been excluded from the established narrative?
- What activities are these 'invisible ones' engaging in while the dominant group seeks to carry out their plans?
- What are the problems that arise as a result of the social processes of dominant and disenfranchised groups?

These are far-reaching and important questions, derived by Hadley in his discussion of GTM and Critical Theory. He offers an account of what Critical Grounded Theory might be, also taking account of the criticism that Critical Grounded Theorists might be 'forcing informant data into preconceived categories'. His additions or enhancements, and those proposed by Hesse-Biber and Flowers (CD:24) and Priya (CD:19), need to 'earn their way' in any specific research project. But it is important that GTM researchers understand that they are there for consideration as part of the method – whether as sensitizing questions or more directly applicable in the research setting itself. These aspects of GTM are particularly important in considering GTM and social justice.

One outcome of such suggestions is that GTM researchers, if and when challenged to articulate one or more 'research questions', now have access to a number of resources to which they can refer in preparing their responses, perhaps pre-empting such challenges and explicitly stating their 'sensitizing questions', derived partly from the examples already given, and also from the research context itself and their own motivations in undertaking the project. (Researcher motivation is an important but largely ignored aspect of research practice – see Bryant, 2017, Chapter 8.)

Note

1   These suggestions can be found in various places in Glaser and Strauss's writings, and are presented together here for convenient reference.

7
GTM, PRAGMATISM AND SOCIAL JUSTICE

GTM has been criticized for leaving things as they are and upholding the status quo, but there are strong grounds to dispute this. Such censure is based on an out-dated and partial understanding of the method; one that particularly fails to take account of the constructivist and Pragmatist aspects that are inherent in the method, albeit that they have only become widely articulated and promulgated since the 1990s. Moreover, the constructivist variant of GTM, while upholding Glaser and Strauss's admonition to keep an open mind in doing research of any kind, makes it clear that all of us, however impartial and unbiased we may try to be and think we are, observe the world and make sense of it through a complex bundle of cognitions, perceptions, expectations, and assumptions. Since it is impossible to evade or escape these, researchers need to recognize and understand this, and proceed accordingly. Again, it is worth quoting Keynes' response to anyone professing themselves immune to such influences: 'Practical men who believe themselves to be quite exempt from any intellectual influence, are usually the slaves of some defunct economist.' The quote continues 'Madmen in authority, who hear voices in the air, are distilling their frenzy from some academic scribbler of a few years back' (Keynes, 1936, pp. 383–384).

Many GTM writers recognize and have responded to this issue, as did Glaser and Strauss, albeit relegating a key statement qualifying their maxim of keeping an open mind to a footnote in *Discovery* that states that 'Of course, the researcher does not approach reality as a *tabula rasa*. He [*sic*] must have a perspective that will help him see relevant data and abstract significant categories from his scrutiny of the data' (Glaser & Strauss, 1967, p. 3).

The phrase 'see relevant data' covers many complex issues which may not have been evident in the 1960s but, given that research is now understood inescapably to encompass issues of power, domination, and hegemony, researchers need constantly to reflect on how their research strategies do or do not engage with these issues. Discussion of research methods has to embrace this; hence the importance of the chapters in *Current Developments* (Bryant & Charmaz, 2019) concerned with indigeneity, critical theory, and feminism, among others, in many cases building upon work published in Denzin's various edited collections (see p. 94).

GTM research has always necessitated paying heed to and engaging with those involved in the research context. Barry Turner stressed this in the 1980s, adding that GTM is an 'approach to qualitative data [that] promotes the development of theoretical accounts which conform closely to the situations being observed, *so that the theory is likely to be intelligible to and usable by those in the situations observed*, and is open to comment and correction by them' (Turner, 1983, pp. 334–335, emphasis added). Which does not imply that the researcher(s) and those embroiled in the context will reach agreement.

Current admonitions, however, go further than this, urging researchers to enter the research arena vigilant and attentive to issues of social justice, which Charmaz has defined as encompassing 'ideas and actions concerning fairness, equity, equality, democratic process, status, and hierarchy, and individual and collective rights and obligations' (Charmaz, 2008b, p. 207). In her recent paper, 'The power of constructivist grounded theory for critical inquiry', Charmaz argues that:

> [T]he constructivist version of grounded theory befits critical qualitative inquiry. ... [it] fosters asking probing questions about the data and scrutinizing the researcher and the research process. Unlike other versions of grounded theory, the constructivist version also locates the research process and product in historical, social, and situational conditions. [It offers] a foundation for bringing grounded theory into critical inquiry and enhancing it. (Charmaz, 2017a, p. 34)

Duckles et al. (CD:31) take up Charmaz's view of critical inquiry as 'embedded in a transformative paradigm that seeks to expose, oppose, and redress forms of oppression, inequality, and injustice' (Charmaz, 2017a, p. 35), stressing that Charmaz also frames (and encourages us to reframe) these abstract processes of justice, injustice, power, and privilege as 'enacted processes, made real through actions performed again and again' (p. 35, italics in original). She proposes that CGT [Constructivist GT] provides the framework and tools to keep our attention as researchers on the constructed, contested and situated nature of these processes.

They argue that this results in part from the influence of Symbolic Interactionism on GTM, since for Charmaz '… symbolic interactionists assume process and explain stability … [offering] an alternative to other social scientific perspectives that assume stability and attempt to explain change. (Charmaz, 2014a, p. 266)'.

Although not all GTM researchers will concur with or adhere to this, Charmaz's position exemplifies a key characteristic of GTM and a criterion for evaluating any Grounded Theory. Developing from her supplementary questions (see above), Charmaz articulates and establishes the foundation for an approach to research that regards social processes as precarious co-constructions, dependent for their continuity on combinations of structure and agency imbricated with each other and with issues such as power, domination, exploitation, and hegemony, also with cultural and political complexities. Far from shoring up the status quo, GTM researchers can and should be working from an orientation that treats stable and enduring social processes as problematic and contested. This draws on and echoes the issues raised in the earlier section on indigeneity.

The 2007 volume touched on some of these issues, for instance in the chapter by O'Neil Green et al. (2007) on 'Grounded theory and racial/ ethnic diversity', but again this is an aspect of GTM that has developed significantly in the intervening years. Bainbridge et al. (CD:30) refer to 'phronetic GTM' – i.e. a form of inquiry that centres on *phronesis*; practical and moral wisdom.

Our phronetic grounded theory approach and transformational grounded theory contributed a decolonizing variation of grounded theory methods and demonstrated its use in the Indigenous Australian and Pacific contexts (Bainbridge, McCalman & Whiteside, 2013; Redman-MacLaren & Mills, 2015). With the exception of Charmaz (2017a), for instance, few theorists have explicitly taken up the proposition and utility of grounded theory as decolonizing tool in research. Yet, grounded theory's pragmatist roots and its commitment to social justice suggest that it can be used purposefully in its intent as a decolonizing method (Charmaz, 2017a). Indeed, grounded theory methods respond to many of the discrete critiques of Western research that Indigenous researchers have proffered in recent decades. We contemplate how the utility of grounded theory methods can provide a fresh perspective and maximize the value of research for Indigenous nations.

They see this as extending constructivist GTM, enabling those working from a constructivist position to building upon this enhanced awareness. In their work they have been concerned to

reflect on our own work to demonstrate that broadening constructivist grounded theory enables it to:

- be ethically-situated and embedded in an explicit moral process philosophy/value position;
- be directly relevant to the lives of the people with whom we work;
- be culturally-sensitive and responsive to people, their priorities and context;
- be reflective and action-oriented;
- work from the strengths of given situations and Indigenous agency;
- be situated as a two-way learning process, explicitly incorporating mutual capacity development;
- value Indigenous knowledge and centre Indigenous voices and experiences;
- explicitly acknowledge and address power dynamics and discourse;
- involve authentic collaboration and trust in the co-creation of knowledge and action;
- integrate Indigenous and Western knowledges;
- study and explicate processes, including why, how and for what purpose;
- capture and explicate in detail a 'big picture' view of research phenomenon that is temporally situated;
- explain what works for whom, under what conditions, through what mechanisms and with what consequences;
- identify points for action, change and intervention.

They also refer to Flyvbjerg's (2001, p. 57)

five value-rational questions for working in a phronetic framework: (1) Where are we going? (2) Who gains and who loses? (3) By which mechanisms of power? (4) Is this desirable? (5) What, if anything, should be done? ... [Adding four more] reflexive, action-oriented questions to generate data: (1) What is the situation? (2) What do we want to change? (3) What is already happening? (4) What's working, what's not, and who is missing out? (5) How can we improve the situation? (Bainbridge et al., CD:30)

To these can be added the feminist sensitizing questions proposed by Hesse-Biber and Flowers (see above and CD:24). The chapters by Denzin (CD:22), and Crossman and Noma (CD:29) develop this perspective, adding further considerations. Denzin quotes from Smith's work (see above) and includes her list of questions that should be posed by all researchers and evaluators.

1. What research do we want done?
2. Who is it for?
3. What difference will it make?
4. Who will carry it out?
5. How do we want the research done?
6. How will we know it is worthwhile?
7. Who will own the research?
8. Who will benefit? (L. Smith, 2000, p. 239).

The chapters by Bainbridge et al. (CD:30), Denzin (CD:22), Duckles et al. (CD:31), and Hadley (CD:28) develop the argument that research in general has to drop the pretence of disinterestedness and impartiality. Quantum physicists have long argued that there is an 'observer effect' when interacting with the physical world; this must be far more pronounced in social settings. I have already pointed to the flaws in the adage that GTM researchers should avoid all preconceptions, arguing that it is far better to try – as far as possible – to articulate one's assumptions and expectations at the outset, leaving it to others to decide the extent to which these influenced the later outcomes. This applies across the research domain, not only to GTM, but the incorporation of the aspirations and concerns given above indicate that GTM is particularly suited as a basis for emancipatory research.

Hadley (CD:28) voices the concerns of those who worry that, for instance, Critical Grounded Theorists are 'forcing informant data into preconceived categories'. Again, it is a case of using sensitizing concepts but ensuring that they have 'earned their way'. The issues and questions listed by Duckles et al. (CD:31), and Hesse-Biber and Flowers (CD:24), and others provide resources for consideration as researchers undertake their inquiries. The chapters by Hadley, Duckles et al., and Carter (CS:27) deal specifically with the ways in which GTM provides a method of critical inquiry when undertaken with a specifically ethical orientation.

Priya (CD:19) similarly makes the case for a form of GTM that starts from a rejection of research as value-neutral and detached, instead seeing

> research interactions [as] ... a site for co-construction that may help bring to the fore an in-depth understanding of experiences from the participant's standpoint through a more flexible procedure of negotiations of meanings or interpretations of shared experience.

In this way, researchers can be aware of, and try to avoid, 'unknowingly [contributing] to legitimizing of social hierarchies that stifle the human voice', instead aiming to recover 'silenced or marginalized voices (Charmaz, 2000, 2017a, 2017b)' (Priya, CD:19).

Duckles et al. (CD:31) refer to Hense and McFerran (2015), who have proposed a critical grounded theory approach that consists of 'iterative cycles in praxis, working with tension and doubt, engaging in democratic collaborations, and ensuring rigor'. Duckles et al. argue that 'these tensions have the potential to lead to more robust and inclusive research directed at meaningful social action and change'. Furthermore, this combination of tension and doubt encourages 'abductive and reflective processes, creating strategies and dialogic spaces to reach into local theories and indigenous ways of knowing and being'.

They explicitly link Pragmatism, concern with social justice, and GTM, quoting Bruce and Bloch (2013), who proposed

> four salient features of pragmatism; 'its emphasis on the *practical* dimensions of inquiry, the *pluralistic* nature of the tools that are used to study phenomena, the *participatory* role of individuals with different perspectives, and the *provisional* nature of inquiry' (p. 28). (Duckles et al., CD:31)

Inquiry is then seen as participatory and active, 'building on Peirce's belief that "the most robust inquiry must involve full participation of all who may have knowledge of the situation"' (Bruce & Bloch, 2013, p. 30).

Stacy Carter (CD:27) offers strong grounds for combining an avowedly ethical stance with GTM:

empirical ethics and value-rich social science can offer three things to grounded theory. The first is an additional depth to data collection, retaining openness but encouraging the presentation of counterfactuals and elicitation of moral reasoning. The second is a new kind of theoretical sensitivity: to normative concepts and questions, which will encourage greater attention to values as significant components in most social and psychological processes. The final benefit is to strengthen the sophisticated approach to the problem of epistemic authority already available in pragmatist traditions.

Carter takes issue with those who argue that the descriptive and the normative – the 'is' and the 'ought' – are distinct. For Carter, they 'are interleaved rather than dichotomous'. This aligns with the view of many Pragmatists, particularly Rorty.

Carter also takes on the issue of how GTM researchers should engage with existing research and literature, explicitly recognizing the role of existing theories and ideas in the generation of grounded theories, then extending this beyond the issue of 'whether existing theory should be used in grounded theorizing (as doing so is unavoidable)', to argue that researchers should be clear in discerning 'which existing theory should be used, and how'.

She notes that recent GTM writing, particularly taking its lead from Charmaz, has focused on 'the moral dimensions of social life, the everyday judgements we make about whether things are right or wrong'. The inevitable result of this is that GTM provides a potent method of research that necessarily addresses ethical and moral issues. Carter welcomes and encourages this, since she is adamant that 'social research should not only describe things or explain how they come to be, but also examine moral judgements, and perhaps even make moral prescriptions'.

IN CONCLUSION

The foregoing discussion developed from reading the submissions to the new *Sage Handbook of Current Developments in Grounded Theory* (Bryant & Charmaz, 2019). These, together with the 2007 *Handbook* (Bryant & Charmaz, 2007a), comprise a rich and challenging set of resources for those with an interest in and/or experience of GTM. The 59 chapters across both volumes encompass discussion of GTM from a wide range of positions, offering extensive material for further reading and encouraging new ideas about topics and approaches to qualitative research, with clear implications, innovations, and challenges for practice and social action: continuing the trend that was set in motion in the 1960s by Glaser and Strauss.

As I read the submitted work, I deliberately used a GTM strategy, studying each chapter in detail, and deriving codes as I did so. In many instances I used verbatim extracts, many of which are included above. The section headings were also for the most part derived in a similar fashion.

As I explained in the introduction, the original title for this discussion was *The Varieties of Grounded Theory Experience*, partly in homage to William James and the original Pragmatists, particularly Peirce and Dewey, but also to underline the ways in which Glaser and Strauss's original work has led to a range of outputs and clarifications that have added considerable depth and profundity to qualitative research and research practice in general. These 'varieties' or variants include the work of Strauss, his later collaboration with Corbin, and also Glaser's individual writings.

The most influential variant, however, stems from the work of Kathy Charmaz, dating from the late 1990s, and incorporating her chapter in the second edition of the *Handbook of Qualitative Research* (2000) and the publication of *Constructing Grounded Theory* (2006). Neither the 2007 *Handbook* nor *Current Developments* could have been assembled and produced without her. Without exception all those approached to contribute a chapter accepted enthusiastically precisely because the invitation came from Kathy. Most of the new contributors to *Current Developments* were her recommendations, and many of the new topics addressed in *Current Developments* emanate directly from her work, particularly on the subject of social justice.

Glaser has always contended, quite correctly, that GTM is itself a grounded theory, and as such it can be judged in the terms that Glaser and Strauss themselves proposed – i.e. *fit, grab, work*, and *modifiability*, to which we must also add Charmaz's criteria of *credibility, originality, resonance*, and *usefulness*. From the evidence of the two *Handbooks*, and the associated resources on which they draw, GTM itself clearly satisfies all these measures. But with the clearly understood caveat that GTM now comprises a 'family' or 'constellation' of orientations and insights that researchers need to approach and appraise drawing on their own *methodological sensitivity*. This latter is a skill that constantly requires exercising and conscious reflection, whether one is an early career doctoral researcher or a well-seasoned and widely-published one.

This may seem onerous to novice researchers as they contend with the plethora of issues that confront anyone entering the field of research and research methods. Anyone in such a position should be able to draw upon one or more mentors to assist, challenge, and support them. Given the earlier discussion of 'minus mentoring', however, this may be particularly problematic for GTM researchers. It is, therefore, important that GTM texts address these issues specifically, with the proviso that differing viewpoints are treated in the manner outlined in Rapoport's rules (see above).

Glaser and Strauss articulated GTM for those new to social science research, offering a basis for novice researchers to feel confident in developing their own conceptualizations and theoretical insights. Yet the founding trilogy – *Awareness* (1965b), *Discovery* (1967), and *Time* (1968) – did not lend itself readily as a set of introductory texts or primers. Strauss's later work, based on his lectures and seminars, began to address this more directly, leading to publication of *Qualitative Analysis for Social Scientists* (1987), and the first two editions of *Basics of Qualitative Research* (Strauss & Corbin, 1990 & 1998). Since the 1990s, Glaser has similarly sought to develop ways in which researchers can be supported and encouraged as they apply GTM in their projects.

Since the publication of Charmaz's *Constructing Grounded Theory*, there has been a welcome flourishing of texts and other resources upon which GTM researchers can draw, and I now offer a brief guide to some of these.

APPENDIX A: KEY RESOURCES AND RECOMMENDED READING

Kathy Charmaz's *Constructing Grounded Theory* (2006, 2014a, and 3rd edition in preparation) provides the best starting point for learning about and understanding GTM, offering an accessible and extended account, and providing a resource that readers can constantly return to as their research develops. In addition, *Awareness* and *Time* provide detailed accounts of the two earliest Grounded Theories, and particular attention should be paid to the appendices which provide succinct methodological overviews (Glaser & Strauss, 1965b, 1968). My own book *Grounded Theory and Grounded Theorizing* (Bryant, 2017) provides some example GTs, and guidance for those preparing their research for doctoral examination and/or submission for possible publication.

Suggestions for further reading on specific topics – listed alphabetically

The chapters in the two *Handbooks* discuss a wealth of resources, to which readers should refer. The collections by Wertz et al. (2011) and Morse et al. (2009 & 2016) also provide important accounts from a variety of perspectives.

Given the importance of certain issues in the foregoing discussion here are some recommendations for initial study of and familiarization with the following topics, the selection is necessarily idiosyncratic and limited to only a few items; readers should refer to the appropriate chapters in both *Handbooks* for further resources.

Abduction

Bryant, A. (2017). *Grounded Theory and Grounded Theorizing: Pragmatism in Research Practice*. Oxford: Oxford University Press. Chapter 13: 'Abduction: No longer an alien concept'.

Plutynski, A. (2011). Four problems of abduction. *Hopos: The Journal of the International Society for the History of Philosophy and Science, 1*(2), 227–248.

Reichertz, J. (2014). Induction, deduction, abduction. In U. Flick (Ed.), *The Sage Handbook of Qualitative Data Analysis* (pp. 123–136). London: Sage.

Sebeok, Th. & Umiker-Sebeok, J. (1979). 'You know my method': A juxtaposition of Charles S. Peirce and Sherlock Holmes. *Semiotica, 26*(2/3), 203–250.

Advice for preparation of PhD theses and article submissions

Bryant, A. (2017). *Grounded Theory and Grounded Theorizing: Pragmatism in Research Practice*. Oxford: Oxford University Press. Chapter 18.

CAQDAS

Friese, Susanne (2016). Qualitative data analysis software: The state of the art. *Special Issue: Qualitative Research in the Digital Humanities*, Bosch, Reinoud (Ed.), *KWALON, 61, 21*(1), 34–45. (See also her chapter).

Hutchisons, Andrew J., Johnston, Lynne H., & Breckon, Jeff D. (2010). Using QSR-NVivo to facilitate the development of a grounded theory project: An account of a worked example. *International Journal of Social Research Methodology, 13*(4), 283–302.

Silver, Christina & Lewins, Ann (2014). *Using Software in Qualitative Research: A Step-By-Step Guide*. London: Sage.

Woolf, Nickolas H. & Silver, Christina (2018). *Qualitative Analysis Using ATLAS.ti/MAXQDA/NVivo: The Five Level QDA Method*. Oxford: Routledge.

Coding and sampling

Charmaz, K. (2014). *Constructing Grounded Theory*. London: Sage. Chapters 5 & 6.

Flick, U. (2014b). *An Introduction to Qualitative Research* (5th edition). London: Sage. Chapter on Sampling.

Morse, Janice M. (2006). Strategies of intraproject sampling. In P. Munhall (Ed.), *Nursing Research: A Qualitative Perspective* (4th edition, pp. 529–540). Boston, MA: Jones & Bartlett.

Morse, J. & Clark, L. (2019). The nuances of theoretical sampling. In A. Bryant & K. Charmaz (Eds.), *The SAGE Handbook of Current Developments in Grounded Theory*. London: Sage. Chapter 7.

Epistemology and ontology

Blaxter, L., Hughes, C., & Tight, M. (2010). *How to Research* (4th edition). Maidenhead, UK: Open University Press.

Bryant, A. (2017). *Grounded Theory and Grounded Theorizing: Pragmatism in Research Practice*. Oxford: Oxford University Press. Chapter 2.

Denzin, Norman K. & Lincoln, Yvonna S. (Eds.) (2000). *Handbook of Qualitative Research* (2nd edition). Thousand Oaks, CA: Sage. Part Two.
Guba, Egon G. & Lincoln, Yvonna S. (1994). Competing paradigms in qualitative research. In Norman K. Denzin & Yvonna S. Lincoln (Eds.), *Handbook of Qualitative Research* (pp. 105–107). Thousand Oaks, CA: Sage.

Metaphors of cognition

Bryant, A. (2006). *Thinking Informatically: Towards a New Understanding of Information, Communication & Technology*. New York and Lewiston, Wales: Edwin Mellen Press. Chapter 3.
Lakoff, G. & Johnson, M. (2003). *Metaphors We Live By*. Chicago, IL: University of Chicago Press.
Reddy, M. (1979). The conduit metaphor: A case of frame conflict in our language about language. In A. Ortony (Ed.), *Metaphor and Thought* (pp. 284–310). Cambridge: Cambridge University Press.

Plans and situated actions

Schön, D. A. (1983). *The Reflective Practitioner: How Professionals Think in Action*. New York: Basic Books.
Suchman, L. (1984). *Plans and Situated Actions: The Problem of Human – Machine Communication*. New York: Cambridge University Press.

Pragmatism

Malachowski, A. (2013). *The Cambridge Companion to Pragmatism* (Cambridge Companions to Philosophy). Cambridge: Cambridge University Press.
Strübing, J. (2019). The Pragmatism of Anselm L. Strauss: Linking theory and method handbook. In A. Bryant & K. Charmaz (Eds.), *The SAGE Handbook of Current Developments in Grounded Theory*. London: Sage. Chapter 2.
Talisse, R. B. & Aikin, S. F. (2008). *Pragmatism: A Guide for the Perplexed*. Guides for the Perplexed series. London: Continuum.

Student accounts – using GTM

Bryant, A. (2017). *Grounded Theory and Grounded Theorizing: Pragmatism in Research Practice*. Oxford: Oxford University Press. Chapter 19.
Grounded Theory Institute – various www.groundedtheory.com/

Theoretical coding

Charmaz, K. (2014). *Constructing Grounded Theory*. London: Sage. Chapters 6, 9 & 11.
Charmaz, K. & Thornberg, R. (2014). Grounded theory and theoretical coding. In U. Flick (Ed.), *The SAGE Handbook of Qualitative Data Analysis*. London: Sage. Chapter 11.

Theoretical saturation

Bryant, A. (2017). *Grounded Theory and Grounded Theorizing: Pragmatism in Research Practice*. Oxford: Oxford University Press. Chapter 12.
Charmaz, K. (2014). *Constructing Grounded Theory*. London: Sage. Chapter 8.

Theoretical sensitivity

Glaser, B. (1978). *Theoretical Sensitivity*. Mill Valley, CA: Sociology Press.
Thistoll, T., Hooper, V., & Pauleen, D. (2016). Acquiring and developing theoretical sensitivity through undertaking a grounded preliminary literature review. *Quality and Quantity, 50*(2), 619–636.

Thinking sociologically

Bauman, Z. & May, T. (2001). *Thinking Sociologically*. New York: Wiley-Blackwell.
Mills, C. W. (1959). *The Sociological Imagination*. Oxford: Oxford University Press.

APPENDIX B: *THE SAGE HANDBOOK OF CURRENT DEVELOPMENTS IN GROUNDED THEORY – LIST OF CHAPTERS*

REFERENCES

Alexander, J. C. (1985). *Neofunctionalism*. London: Sage.

Austin, J. L. (1962). *How to Do Things with Words*. (William James Lectures). Oxford: Oxford University Press.

Bacharach, S. (1989). Organizational theories: Some criteria for evaluation. *Academy of Management Review, 14,* 496–515.

Bainbridge, R., McCalman, J., & Whiteside, M. (2013). Being, knowing, and doing: A phronetic approach to constructing grounded theory with Aboriginal Australian partners. *Qualitative Health Research, 23*(2), 275–288.

Banks, M. (2001). *Visual Methods in Social Research*. London: Sage.

Bauman, Z. (1971). *Community: Seeking Safety in an Insecure World*. Cambridge: Polity Press.

Bauman, Z. & May, T. (2001). *Thinking Sociologically*. New York: Wiley-Blackwell.

Becker, H. S., Geer, B., Hughes, E. C., & Strauss, A. L. (1961). *Boys in White: Student Culture in Medical School*. Chicago, IL: University of Chicago Press.

Benoliel, J. Q. (1984). Advancing nursing science: Qualitative approaches. *Western Journal of Nursing Research, 63*(3), 1–8.

Benoliel, J. Q. (1996). Grounded theory and nursing knowledge. *Qualitative Health Research, 6*(3), 406–428.

Bishop, R. (1998). Freeing ourselves from neo-colonial domination in research: A Maori approach to creating knowledge. *International Journal of Qualitative Studies in Education, 11,* 199–219.

Blumer, H. (1954). What is wrong with social theory? *American Sociological Review, 19,* 3–10.

Blumer, H. (1969). What is wrong with social theory? In Herbert Blumer (1969/1986), *Symbolic Interactionism* (pp. 140–152). Berkeley, CA: University of California Press. Originally published in Vol. *XIX* in *The American Sociological Review*.

Bruce, B. C. & Bloch, N. (2013). Pragmatism and community inquiry: A case study of community-based learning. *Education and Culture, 29*(1), 27–45.

Bryant, A. (2002). Re-grounding grounded theory. *Journal of Information Technology Theory and Application, 4,* 25–42.

Bryant, A. (2006). *Thinking Informatically: Towards a New Understanding of Information, Communication & Technology*. New York and Lewiston, Wales: Edwin Mellen Press.

Bryant, A. (2009). Grounded theory and pragmatism: The curious case of Anselm Strauss. *Forum Qualitative Sozialforschung / Forum: Qualitative Social Research, 10*(3), Article 2, September.

Bryant, A. (2014). Thinking about The Information Age. *Informatics*, *1*, 190–195.

Bryant, A. (2017). *Grounded Theory and Grounded Theorizing: Pragmatism in Research Practice*. Oxford: Oxford University Press.

Bryant, A. (2019). Senior Editor's introduction. *The Sage Handbook of Current Developments in Grounded Theory*. London: Sage.

Bryant, A., Black, A., Land, F., & Porra, J. (2013). Information systems history: What is history what is IS history What IS history and why even bother with history. *Journal of Information Technology*, *28*(1), 1–17.

Bryant, A. & Charmaz, K. (Eds.) (2007a). *The Sage Handbook of Grounded Theory*. London: Sage.

Bryant, A. & Charmaz, K. (2007b). Grounded theory research: Method and practices, Editors' Introduction. In A. Bryant & K. Charmaz (Eds.), *The Sage Handbook of Grounded Theory* (pp. 1–28). London: Sage.

Bryant, A. & Charmaz, K. (2007c). Grounded theory in historical perspective: An epistemological account. In A. Bryant & K. Charmaz (Eds.), *The Sage Handbook of Grounded Theory* (pp. 31–57). London: Sage.

Bryant, A. & Charmaz, K. (Eds.) (2019). *The Sage Handbook of Current Developments in Grounded Theory*. London: Sage.

Bryant, A. & Raja, U. (2014). In the realm of Big Data. *First Monday*, *19*(2&3), http://firstmonday. org/article/view/4991/3822

Burawoy, M. (1991). The extended case method. In M. Burawoy, A. Burton, A. Ferguson, K. Fox, J. Gamson, N. Gartrell, L. Hurst, C. Kurzman, L. Salzinger, J. Schiffman & S. Ui (Eds.), *Ethnography Unbound: Power and Resistance in the Modern Metropolis* (pp. 271–287). Berkeley & Los Angeles, CA: University of California Press.

Burawoy, M. (1998). The extended case method. *Social Theory*, *16*(1), March.

Butler, J. (2013). Judith Butler on gender as 'performed' or 'performative'. *Critical Theory*, posted 8 November, https://my.vanderbilt.edu/criticaltheory fall13/2013/11/judith-butler-on-gender-as-performed-or-performative/

Camus, A. (2000 [1951]). *The Rebel*. Harmondsworth: Penguin.

Castells, M. (2009). *Communication Power*. Oxford: Oxford University Press.

Castells, M. (2016). A sociology of power: My intellectual journey. *Annual Review of Sociology*, *42*, 1–19.

Charmaz, K. (1983). Loss of self: A fundamental form of suffering in the chronically ill. *Sociology of Health and Illness*, *5*(2).

Charmaz, K. (2000). Grounded theory: Objectivist and constructivist methods. In N. K. Denzin & Y. S. Lincoln (Eds.), *Handbook of Qualitative Research* (2nd edition, pp. 509–535). Thousand Oaks, CA: Sage.

Charmaz, K. (2006). *Constructing Grounded Theory*. Thousand Oaks, CA: Sage.

Charmaz, K. (2008a). Constructionism and the grounded theory method. In J. A. Holstein & J. F. Gubrium (Eds.), *Handbook of Constructionist Research* (pp. 397–412). New York: Guilford Press.

Charmaz, K. (2008b). Grounded theory in the 21st Century: Applications for advancing social justice studies. In N. K. Denzin & Y. S. Lincoln (Eds.), *Strategies of Quaitatve Inquiry*, (3rd edition). Thousand Oaks, CA: Sage.

Charmaz, K. (2014a). *Constructing Grounded Theory* (2nd edition). Thousand Oaks, CA: Sage.

Charmaz, K. (2014b). Grounded theory in global perspective: Reviews by international researchers. *Qualitative Inquiry, 20*(9), 1074–1084.

Charmaz, K. (2017a). The power of constructivist grounded theory for critical inquiry. *Qualitative Inquiry, 23*(1), 34–45.

Charmaz, K. (2017b). Special Invited Paper: Continuities, contradictions, and critical inquiry in grounded theory. *International Journal of Qualitative Methods, 16*(1).

Charmaz, K. & Keller, R. (2016). A personal journey with grounded theory methodology: Kathy Charmaz in conversation with Reiner Keller. *Forum Qualitative Sozialforschung / Forum: Qualitative Social Research, 17*(1), Article 16, January.

Clarke, A. (2005). *Situational Analysis: Grounded Theory after the Postmodern Turn.* Thousand Oaks, CA: Sage.

Clarke, A. (2007). Grounded theorizing using situational analysis. In A. Bryant & K. Charmaz (Eds.), *The Sage Handbook of Grounded Theory* (pp. 363–397). London: Sage.

Clarke, A. (2009). From grounded theory to situational analysis: What's new? Why? How? In J. M. Morse, P. N. Stern, J. Corbin, B. Bowers, K. Charmaz, & A. E. Clarke (Eds.), *Developing Grounded Theory: The Second Generation* (pp. 194–235). Walnut Creek, CA: Left Coast Press.

Clarke, A. (Ed.) (2015). *Situational Analysis in Practice.* London: Routledge.

Clarke, A., Friese, C., & Washburn, R. S. (2017). *Situational Analysis: Grounded Theory after the Postmodern Turn* (2nd edition). Thousand Oaks, CA: Sage.

Clarke, A. & Keller, R. (2014). Engaging complexities: Working against simplification as an agenda for qualitative research today. Adele Clarke in conversation with Reiner Keller. *Forum Qualitative Sozialforschung/Forum: Qualitative Social Research, 15*(2).

Corbin, J. (2011). *Grounded Theory Methodology.* Studienbrief der Fern Universität Hagen. Available at: https://vu.fernuni-hagen.de/lvuweb/lvu/file/.../33800-vorschau.pdf

Corbin, J. & Strauss, A. L. (1988). *Unending Work and Care: Managing Chronic Illness at Home.* San Francisco, CA: Jossey-Bass.

Corbin, J. & Strauss, A. L. (1990, 2008 & 2015). *Basics of Qualitative Research: Techniques and Procedures for Developing Grounded Theory* (1st, 3rd & 4th editions). Thousand Oaks, CA: Sage.

Covan, E. K. (2007). The discovery of grounded theory in practice: The legacy of multiple mentors. In A. Bryant & K. Charmaz (Eds.), *The Sage Handbook of Grounded Theory* (pp. 58–93). Thousand Oaks, CA: Sage.

Denzin, N. K. (1970). *The Research Act: A Theoretical Introduction to Sociological Methods.* Chicago, London: Aldine

Denzin, N. K. (2003) *Performance Ethnography: The Politics and Pedagogies of Culture.* London: Sage

Denzin, N. K. & Giardina, M. D. (Eds.). (2009). *Qualitative Inquiry and Social Justice.* Walnut Creek: Left Coast Press

Denzin, N. K. & Giardina, M. D. (eds.) (2010). *Qualitative Inquiry and Human Rights.* Walnut Creek: Left Coast Press

Denzin, N. K., Lincoln, Y. S. & Smith, L. T. (2008) *Handbook of Critical Indigenous Inquiry*. Thousand Oaks: Sage.

Denzin, N. K. & Lincoln, Y. S. (Eds.) (1994, 2000, 2001, 2005 & 2017). *The Sage Handbook of Qualitative Research* (1st, 2nd, 3rd, 4th, & 5th editions). Thousand Oaks, CA: Sage.

Dewey, John (1929). *Experience and Nature*. Chicago, IL: Open Court Publishing.

Dewey, John (1938). *Logic, the Theory of Inquiry*. New York: Holt, Rinehart and Winston.

Dey, I. (1999). *Grounding Grounded Theory: Guidelines for Qualitative Inquiry*. San Diego, CA: Academic Press.

Dey, I. (2007). Grounding categories. In A. Bryant & K. Charmaz (Eds.), *The Sage Handbook of Grounded Theory* (pp. 167–190). London: Sage.

Dick, B., Stringer, E., & Huxham, C. (2009). Theory in action. *Action Research, 7*(1), 5–12.

Eisenstadt, S. N. (2003). *Comparative Civilizations & Multiple Modernities*. Leiden: Brill.

Fine, G. (1993). The sad demise, mysterious disappearance and glorious triumph of symbolic interactionism. *Annual Review of Sociology, 19*, 61–68.

Flick, U. (2008a). *Designing Qualitative Research*. London: Sage.

Flick, U. (2008b). *Managing Qualitative Research*. London: Sage.

Flick, U. (Ed.) (2014a). *The SAGE Handbook of Qualitative Data Analysis*. London: Sage.

Flick, U. (2014b). *An Introduction to Qualitative Research* (5th edition). London: Sage.

Flick, U. (2015). Qualitative Inquiry – 2.0 at 20? Developments, trends, and challenges for the politics of research. *Qualitative Inquiry, 21*(7), 599–608.

Flyvbjerg, B. (2001). *Making Social Science Matter: Why Social Inquiry Fails and How it Can Succeed Again*. Cambridge: Cambridge University Press.

Foucault, M. (2004). *Geschichte der Gouvernementalität*. Frankfurt am Main: Suhrkamp.

Friese, Susanne (2016). Qualitative data analysis software: The state of the art. *Special Issue: Qualitative Research in the Digital Humanities*, Bosch, Reinoud (Ed.), KWALON, 61, *21*(1), 34–45.

Gerhardt, U. (1976). Krankenkarriere und Existenzbelastung. *Zeitschrift für Soziologie, 5*(3), 215–236.

Gibson, B. (2007). Accommodating grounded theory. In A. Bryant & K. Charmaz (Eds.), *The Sage Handbook of Grounded Theory* (pp. 436–453). London: Sage.

Gibson, B. & Hartman, J. (2014). *Rediscovering Grounded Theory*. London: Sage.

Gilgun, J. (1993). Grounded theory and dimensional analysis: An interview with Leonard Schatzman. Available at: https://janegilgun.wordpress.com/2012/03/06/transcript-of-an-interview-with-leonard-schatzman/

Gilgun, J. F. (1999). Methodological pluralism and qualitative family research. In Suzanne K. Steinmetz, Marvin B. Sussman, & Gary W. Peterson (Eds.), *Handbook of Marriage and the Family* (2nd edition, pp. 219–261). New York: Plenum.

Gilgun, J. F. (2005). Qualitative research and family psychology. *Journal of Family Psychology, 19*(1), 40–50.

Gilgun, J. F. (2016). *Deductive qualitative analysis and the search for black swans*. Paper presented at the Pre-conference Workshop on Theory Construction and Research Methodology, National Council on Family Relations, Minneapolis, MN, November 1.

Glaser, B. G. (1978). *Theoretical Sensitivity*. Mill Valley, CA: Sociology Press.

Glaser, B. G. (1992). *Emergence vs. Forcing: Basics of Grounded Theory Analysis*. Mill Valley, CA: Sociology Press.

Glaser, B. G. (1998). *Doing Grounded Theory: Issues and discussions*. Mill Valley, CA: Sociology Press.

Glaser, B. G. (2002). Constructivist grounded theory? *Forum Qualitative Sozialforschung / Forum: Qualitative Social Research, 3*(3).

Glaser, B. G. (2004). Remodeling grounded theory. *Forum Qualitative Sozialforschung / Forum: Qualitative Social Research, 5*(2) Article 4 – May. [Barney G. Glaser with the assistance of Judith Holton]. Available at: www.qualitative-research.net/index.php/fqs/article/view/607/1315

Glaser, B. G. (2008). *Doing Quantitative Grounded Theory*. Mill Valley, CA: Sociology Press.

Glaser, B. G. (2009). *Jargonizing: Using the Grounded Theory Vocabulary*. Mill Valley, CA: Sociology Press.

Glaser, B. G. (2014). Applying grounded theory. *Grounded Theory Review, 13*(1), June.

Glaser, B. G. & Strauss, A. L. (1965a). Discovery of substantive theory: A basic strategy underlying qualitative research. *American Behavioral Scientist, 8*(6), 5–12.

Glaser, B. G. & Strauss, A. L. (1965b). *Awareness of Dying*. Chicago, IL: Aldine.

Glaser, B. G. & Strauss, A. L. (1967). *The Discovery of Grounded Theory*. Chicago, IL: Aldine.

Glaser, B. G. & Strauss, A. L. (1968). *Time for Dying*. Chicago, IL: Aldine.

Glaser, B. G. & Strauss, A. L. (1971). *Status Passage*. Chicago, IL: Aldine.

Goffman, E. (1959). *The Presentation of Self in Everyday Life*. New York: Doubleday.

Gouldner, A. (1973). Romanticism and Classicism: Deep structures in social science. In A. Gouldner, *For Sociology: Renewal and Critique in Sociology Today*. New York: Basic Books. Available at: www.autodidactproject.org/other/gouldner5.html

Gregor, S. (2006). The nature of theory in information systems. *MIS Quarterly, 30*(3), 611–642.

Hammersley, M. (2004). Analytic induction. In Michael S. Lewis-Beck, Alan Bryman, & Tim Futing Liao (Eds.), *The SAGE Encyclopedia of Social Science Research Methods* (pp. 16–18). London: Sage.

Hammersley, M. (2010). A historical and comparative note on the relationship between analytic induction and grounded theorising. *Forum Qualitative Sozialforschung / Forum: Qualitative Social Research, 11*(42).

Hammersley, M. (2011). On Becker's studies of marijuana use as an example of analytic induction. *Philosophy of the Social Sciences, 41*(4).

Hammersley, M. & Atkinson, P. (1995). *Ethnography: Principles in Practice* (2nd edition). London: Routledge.

Hempel, C. (1952). *Fundamentals of Concept Formation in Empirical Science*. Chicago, IL: University of Chicago Press.

Hense, C. & McFerran, K. S. (2015). Toward a critical grounded theory. *Qualitative Research Journal*, *16*(4), 402–416.

Hernandez, C. A. (2009). Theoretical coding in grounded theory methodology. *Grounded Theory Review*, *8*(3), November. Available at: http://groundedtheoryreview.com/2009/11/30/theoretical-coding-in-grounded-theory-methodology/

Hirschman, A. O. (1990 [1970]). *Exit, Voice and Loyalty: Responses to Decline in Firms, Organizations and States* (1990 edition). Cambridge, MA: Harvard University Press.

Israel, B. A., Eng, E., Schultz, A. J., & Parker, E. A. (2005). *Methods in Community-based Participatory Research for Health*. San Francisco, CA: Jossey-Bass.

James, W. (1902). *The Varieties of Religious Experience*. London: Longmans.

James, W. (2000). *Pragmatism and Other Writings*. Penguin Classics. Harmondsworth: Penguin.

Kearney, M. (2007). From the sublime to the meticulous. In A. Bryant & K. Charmaz (Eds.), *The Sage Handbook of Grounded Theory*. London: Sage.

Kelle, U. (2007). The development of categories: Different approaches in grounded theory. In A. Bryant & K. Charmaz (Eds.), *The SAGE Handbook of Grounded Theory* (pp. 191–213). London: Sage.

Kennedy, B. & Thornberg, R. (2018). Deduction, induction, and abduction. In U. Flick (Ed.), *The SAGE Handbook of Qualitative Data Collection* (pp. 49–64). London: Sage.

Keynes, J. M. (1936). *The General Theory of Employment, Interest and Money*. London: Macmillan.

Kincheloe, J. & McLaren, P. (2000). Rethinking critical theory and qualitative research. In N. Denzin & Y. Lincoln (Eds.), *Handbook of Qualitative Research* (2nd edition, pp. 279–313). Thousand Oaks, CA: Sage.

Kuhn, T. S. (1962 & 1970). *The Structure of Scientific Revolutions*. Chicago, IL: University of Chicago Press.

Lakoff, G. & Johnson, M. (2003). *Metaphors We Live By*. Chicago, IL: University of Chicago Press.

Layder, D. (1993). *New Strategies in Social Research: An Introduction and Guide*. Cambridge: Polity Press.

Lincoln, Y. S. & Guba, E. G. (2013). *The Constructivist Credo*. Walnut Creek, CA: Left Coast Press.

Lindesmith, R. & Strauss, A. L. (2009 [1949]). *Social Psychology*. New York: The Dryden Press.

Lofland, J. (1980). Reminiscences of Chicago: The Blumer-Hughes Talk. *Urban Life*, *9*, 251–289.

Maines, D., Sugrue, N., & M. Katovich (1983). The sociological import of G. H. Mead's Theory of the Past. *American Sociological Review*, *48*(2), 161–173.

Mead, G. H. (1934). *Mind, Self & Society from the Standpoint of a Social Behaviorist*. Chicago, IL: University of Chicago Press.

Mead, G. H. (1959 [1932]). *The Philosophy of the Present*. La Salle, IL: Open Court Publishing.

Merton, R. K. (1949). On sociological theories of the middle range. In R. K. Merton, *Social Theory and Social Structure* (pp. 39–53). NewYork: Simon & Schuster.

Merton, R. K. (1957). *Social Theory and Social Structure*. Glencoe, IL: Free Press.

Minkler, M. & Wallerstein, N. (2011). Introduction to community-based participatory research: New issues and emphases. In M. Minkler & N. Wallerstein (Eds.), *Community-Based Participatory Research for Health: From Process to Outcomes* (pp. 5–23). Hoboken, NJ: Jossey-Bass.

Morrison, D. E. (1978). Kultur and culture: The case of Theodor W. Adorno and Paul F. Lazarsfeld. *Social Research, 45*(2), Summer.

Morse, J., Stern, P. N., Corbin, J., Bowers, B., Charmaz, K., & Clarke, A. E. (2009 & 2016). *Developing Grounded Theory: The Second Generation*. Walnut Creek, CA: Left Coast Press, 2009; London: Routledge, 2016.

Nagel, D. A., Burns, V. F., Tilley, C., & Aubin, D. (2015). When novice researchers adopt constructivist grounded theory: Navigating less travelled paradigmatic and methodological paths in PhD dissertation work. *International Journal of Doctoral Studies, 10*, 365–383.

O'Neil Green, D., Creswell, J. W., Shope, R. J., & Plano Clark, V. L. (2007). Grounded theory and racial/ethnic diversity. In A. Bryant & K. Charmaz (Eds.), *The Sage Handbook of Grounded Theory* (pp. 472–492). London: Sage.

Parker, R. & Pollock, G. (1981/1995). *Old Mistresses: Women, Art and Ideology*. London: Pandora.

Parsons, T. (1937). *The Structure of Social Action*. New York: Free Press.

Peirce, C. S. (1986). *Philosophical Writings*. New York: Dover.

Peirce, C. S. (1992). *Reasoning and the Logic of Things*. Edited by K. L. Ketner. Cambridge, MA: Harvard University Press.

Polanyi, M. (1958). *Personal Knowledge: Towards a Post-Critical Philosophy*. Chicago, IL: University of Chicago Press.

Polanyi, M. (1966). *The Tacit Dimension*. Chicago, IL: University of Chicago Press.

Quint, J. C. (1965). Institutionalized practices of information control. *Psychiatry Interpersonal and Biological Processes, 28*(2).

Quint, J. C. (1967). *The Nurse and the Dying Patient*. New York: Macmillan.

Ragin, C. (1994). *Constructing Social Research*. Thousand Oaks, CA: Pine Forge Press.

Ralph, N., Birks, M., & Chapman, Y. (2015). The methodological dynamism of grounded theory. *International Journal of Qualitative Methods, 14*(4), 1–6.

Reason, P. & Bradbury-Huang, H. (2015). *Action Research Handbook* (2nd edition). London: Sage.

Reddy, M. (1979). The conduit metaphor: A case of frame conflict in our language about language. In A. Ortony (Ed.), *Metaphor and Thought* (pp. 164–201). Cambridge: Cambridge University Press.

Redman-MacLaren, M. & Mills, J. (2015). Transformational grounded theory: Theory, voice, and action. *International Journal of Qualitative Methods, 14*(3).

Reichertz, J. (2007). Abduction: The logic of discovery in grounded theory. In A. Bryant & K. Charmaz (Eds.), *The Sage Handbook of Grounded Theory* (pp. 214–228). London: Sage.

Rorty, R. (1977). Dewey's metaphysics. In Steven M. Cahn (Ed.), *New Studies in the Philosophy of John Dewey*. Hanover, NH: University Press of New England.

Rorty, R. (1989). *Contingency, Irony, and Solidarity*. Cambridge: Cambridge University Press.

Rorty, R. (1991). *Objectivity, Relativism and Truth*. Cambridge: Cambridge University Press.

Rorty, R. (1999). Relativism: Finding and making. In R. Rorty, *Philosophy and Social Hope*. London and New York: Penguin.

Rorty, R. (2007). Cultural politics and the question of the existence of God. In R. Rorty, *Philosophy as Cultural Politics: Philosophical Papers Volume 4*. Cambridge: Cambridge University Press.

Saldana, J. (2015). *The Coding Manual for Qualitative Researchers* (3rd edition). London: Sage.

Sartwell, C. (2015). Philosophy returns to the real world. *New York Times*, Opionator blogs, 13 April. Available at: http://opinionator.blogs.nytimes.com/2015/04/13/philosophy-returns-to-the-real-world

Schön, D. A. (1983). *The Reflective Practitioner: How Professionals Think in Action*. New York: Basic Books.

Searle, J. (1969). *Speech Acts: An Essay in the Philosophy of Language*. Cambridge: Cambridge University Press.

Shank, G. (1987). Abductive strategies in educational research. *American Journal of Semiotics*, 5(2), 275–290.

Shank, G. (1998). The extraordinary ordinary powers of abductive reasoning. *Theory & Psychology*, 8(6), 841–860.

Shank, G. & Cunningham, D. J. (1996). Modeling the six modes of Peircean abduction for educational purposes. Paper presented at the annual meeting of the Midwest AI and Cognitive Science Conference, Bloomington, IN. Online address for MAICS 1996 Proceedings available at: www.cs.indiana.edu/event/maics96/Proceedings/shank.html

Smith, L. T. (2000). Kupapa Maori research. In Marie Battiste (Ed.), *Reclaiming Indigenous Voice and Vision* (pp. 225–247). Vancouver: UBC Press.

Smith, L. T. (2005). On tricky ground: Researching the native in the age of uncertainty. In N. K. Denzin & Y. S. Lincoln (Eds.), *Handbook of Qualitative Research* (3rd edition, pp. 85–108). Thousand Oaks, CA: Sage.

Smith, L. T. (2012). *Decolonizing Methodologies: Research and Indigenous Peoples* (2nd editon). London: Zed Books.

Stainton-Rogers, W. (2003). *Social Psychology: Experimental and Critical Approaches*. Maidenhead: Open University Press.

Stanford Encyclopedia of Philosophy (n.d.). https://plato.stanford.edu. Entries on `genealogy'; `Romanticism'; `Fleck'; `emergence'.

Stern, P. N. (2007). On solid ground: Essential properties for growing grounded theory. In A. Bryant & K. Charmaz (Eds.), *The Sage Handbook of Grounded Theory* (pp. 114–126). London: Sage.

Stern, P. N. (2012). Jeanne Quint Benoliel. *Qualitative Health Research, 22* (November), 1580–1581.

Strauss, A. L. (1959). *Mirrors and Masks: The Search for Identity*. Medicine in Society Series. London: Martin Robertson & Co.

Strauss, A. L. (1964). *Psychiatric Ideologies and Institutions*. New York: Free Press.

Strauss, A. L. (1987). *Qualitative Analysis for Social Scientists*. Cambridge: Cambridge University Press.

Strauss, A. L. (1993). *Continual Permutations of Action: Communication and Social Order*. New York: W. de Gruyter.

Strauss, A. L. & Corbin, J. (1990 & 1998). *Basics of Qualitative Research* (1st & 2nd editions). Newbury Park, CA: Sage.

Strauss, A. & Corbin, J. (1994). Grounded theory methodology: An overview. In N. K. Denzin & Y. S. Lincoln (Eds.), *Handbook of Qualitative Research* (pp. 273–285). Thousand Oaks, CA: Sage.

Strauss, A. L., Glaser, B. G., & Quint, J. (1964). The Nonaccountability of Terminal Care. *Hospitals, 38*(January), 73–87.

Strauss, A. L., Schatzman, L., Bucher, R., Erlich, D., & Sabshin, M. (1963). The hospital and its negotiated order. In E. Freidson (Ed.), *The Hospital in Modern Society* (pp. 147–163). New York: Free Press.

Strübing, J. (2007). *Anselm Strauss*. Constance: UVK.

Suchman, L. (1984). *Plans and Situated Actions: The Problem of Human–Machine Communication*. New York: Cambridge University Press.

Tavory, I. & Timmermans, S. (2009). Two cases of ethnography: Grounded theory and the extended case method. *Ethnography, 10*, 243–263.

Turner, B. (1983). The use of grounded theory for the qualitative analysis of organizational behaviour. *Journal of Management Studies, 20*(3), 333–348.

Wacquant, L. (2002). Scrutinizing the street: Poverty, morality, and the pitfalls of urban ethnography. *American Journal of Sociology, 107*(6), May.

Weick, K. E. (1995). What theory is not, theorizing IS. *Administrative Science Quarterly, 40*, 385–390.

Wertz, F. J., Charmaz, K., McMullen, L. M., Josselson, R., Anderson, R., & McSpadden, E. (2011). *Five Ways of Doing Qualitative Analysis: Phenomenological Psychology, Grounded Theory, Discourse Analysis, Narrative Research, and Intuitive Inquiry*. New York: Guilford Press.

Wiener, C. (2007). Making teams work in conducting ground theory. In A. Bryant & K. Charmaz (Eds.), *The Sage Handbook of Grounded Theory* (pp. 293–310). London: Sage.

Wittgenstein, L. (n.d.). Aphorisms 66 and 67. *Philosophical Investigations*. Available at: http://users.rcn.com/athbone/lw65-69c.htm

Wittgenstein, L. (2001 [1953]). *Philosophical Investigations*. Oxford: Blackwell.

INDEX